TEACHING THE PRIMARY CURRICULUM OUTDOORS

TEACHING THE PRIMARY CURRICULUM OUTDOORS

LEARNING THROUGH LANDSCAPES

A SAGE company
2455 Teller Road
Thousand Oaks, California 91320
(0800)233-9936
www.corwin.com

SAGE Publications Ltd
1 Oliver's Yard
55 City Road
London EC1Y 1SP

SAGE Publications India Pvt Ltd
B 1/I 1 Mohan Cooperative Industrial Area
Mathura Road
New Delhi 110 044

SAGE Publications Asia-Pacific Pte Ltd
3 Church Street
#10-04 Samsung Hub
Singapore 049483

© 2022 Learning Through Landscapes

First published in 2022

Apart from any fair dealing for the purposes of research, private study, or criticism or review, as permitted under the Copyright, Designs and Patents Act, 1988, this publication may not be reproduced, stored or transmitted in any form, or by any means, without the prior permission in writing of the publisher, or in the case of reprographic reproduction, in accordance with the terms of licences issued by the Copyright Licensing Agency. Enquiries concerning reproduction outside those terms should be sent to the publisher.

Editor: Amy Thornton
Senior project editor: Chris Marke
Project management: River Editorial
Marketing manager: Dilhara Attygalle
Cover design: Wendy Scott
Typeset by: C&M Digitals (P) Ltd, Chennai, India
Printed in the UK

Library of Congress Control Number: 2022930475

British Library Cataloguing in Publication Data

A catalogue record for this book is available from the British Library

ISBN 978-1-5297-8043-7
ISBN 978-1-5297-8044-4 (pbk)

At SAGE we take sustainability seriously. Most of our products are printed in the UK using responsibly sourced papers and boards. When we print overseas we ensure sustainable papers are used as measured by the PREPS grading system. We undertake an annual audit to monitor our sustainability.

Contents

Preface vii
Acknowledgements viii
About this book ix
About learning through landscapes xi

PART 1   Practicalities 1

1 Taking your learning outdoors 3

2 Some inspiration from schools 8

3 Sustainability and climate change 12

4 Tackling the challenges and obstacles 13

5 Accessibility and inclusion 24

6 Making it last 26

7 Myth busting 27

8 Making plans 28

PART 2   Activities for curriculum teaching 29

9 Language and literacy 31

10 Maths and numeracy 63

11 Science 94

12 Humanities 129

13 The arts 156

14 Technology including cooking 173

PART 3 More practical activities and resources   **181**

15 Quick activity ideas and techniques   183

16 Themes   197

17 Other useful resources   234

Index   237

Preface

By Carley Sefton, CEO of Learning through Landscapes

Most workdays are good, some are great and others are fantastic, but the day I opened the email asking our team to write this book has to be one of the best. In the past 30 years Learning through Landscapes (LtL) has published many books on outdoor learning, but I don't think any have been more needed or timely than this one.

As I write this in late 2021, we are still grappling with the ongoing coronavirus (COVID-19) pandemic. At times over the last eighteen months I think we have all struggled to see any positives in this situation, but I believe one of the few good things to come out of this strange time has been an increase in our understanding of the importance of time outdoors, especially for children and young people. However, from speaking to teachers and educators who want to take more lessons outside, I'm aware that many have struggled to know where to start when they are already under so much pressure.

Learning through Landscapes is unique because we put education first with nearly all our team being teachers or educationalists. This contrasts with other organisations who prioritise environmental themes. We therefore truly understand what it's like to work in schools and are very aware of the daily challenges many teachers face, including a lack of time and resources.

This book has been written with the aim of overcoming these hurdles. It will allow you to introduce curriculum-linked lessons into your daily practice at your own pace, using all the skills you already have. We want you to think of these lessons as doing something differently rather than learning something new; taking classes outdoors can simply give you a fresh perspective on delivering lessons that you may have been teaching for years.

But as you introduce more outdoor learning to your school day you'll find that it does so much more than just bring the curriculum to life: spending time outside has proven mental health and wellbeing benefits, not only for your pupils but for you as well!

I hope this book will support you on your outdoor learning journey, enabling you to enjoy daily time outside with your class throughout every season of the year. By using this book to connect yourself and your pupils to the natural environment, you will discover those magical moments of awe and wonder that only time in nature can provide.

> *If children don't grow up knowing about nature and appreciating it,*
> *they will not understand it.*
> *And if they don't understand it, they won't protect it.*
> *And if they don't protect it, who will?*
>
> (Sir David Attenborough,
> Founding Board Member and Patron of Learning through Landscapes)

Acknowledgements

As with most charities, it took a brilliant team fuelled by passion and expertise to bring this book together.

Thank you to all at Learning through Landscapes who helped write, proof and bring together this book, especially: Alex, Charly, Cindy, Dawn, Graham, Hafsah, Kirsty, Jane, Marianne, Matt, Ruth and Steve.

To all the children who checked to make sure that all the resources are interesting and enjoyable:

Aiha, Caden, Cole, Daniel, Diya, Evie, Farshad, Felix, Hadiya, Harvey, Hasnath, Jessica, Kelsea, Kobe, Lily-Mai, Lyla, Maisie, Mason, Mohammed, Ophia, Oscar C, Oscar W, Phoebe, Polly, Robbie, Ryan-Lee, Samuel, Tasnim, Tyler, Xanthe, Yorham.

Our amazing photographers Gemma at Gemma Brunton Photography and Simon at Simon Hadley Photography.

A huge thank you to The Polygon School, Southampton and Beaumont Lodge Neighbourhood Association, Leicester for allowing us to use their beautiful spaces to test our resources.

To all at SAGE Publishing especially Amy Thornton for supporting us so well through the process

And with special thanks to Mary Jackson whose life work is to improve the use of school grounds across the world. Her expertise and passion for outdoor learning is clear on every page.

About this book

Welcome to *Teaching the Primary Curriculum Outdoors*, we hope you will enjoy exploring the book, find new ideas for teaching outdoors and try them out with your own pupils.

There are a number of sections to this book. We start by giving you an overview of why we believe teaching outside can really engage your pupils, help them connect more with new learning and reinforce principles they have been looking at in the classroom.

We then help you to look at your own practice, address questions and worries you may have about teaching outside, and help you plan your next steps in your journey.

But the bulk of the book is the lesson activities section. There are over 100 ideas for taking lesson activities outside from ten-minute energisers to extended themes across different curriculum areas, and everywhere in between. This is not a book that tells you to be outside for every lesson, we don't believe you should. Instead when you look at your schemes of work and lesson plans we want you to think, 'Would going outside add something to this for my pupils?' We believe that this is often the case and are sure that, when you start to take more learning outside, you will believe it too.

> At Learning through Landscapes we are about children and education first; we just believe that some things can be taught better outside!

About Learning through Landscapes

Learning through Landscapes is the UK's national school grounds charity. Since 1990 we have been helping schools, and those who work in and for them, to make the most of their grounds for learning, play and connection with nature.

Our vision is a society where the benefits of regular time outdoors are valued and appreciated, and outdoor learning, play and connection with nature is recognised as a fundamental part of education, at every stage, for every child and young person.

We do this by advocating the benefits of outdoor learning and play at school and preschool, inspiring and enabling the design and development of outdoor environments to support children's development, as well as giving teachers and early years practitioners the confidence, ideas and skills they need to make better use of outdoor spaces.

This book is just one way we support schools with outdoor learning. We also run training, provide funding and resources through grant programmes and run projects that engage pupils, the school and wider community. We work with other organisations and agencies to advocate outdoor learning and play and to ensure that school grounds are seen as valued spaces for all children and young people.

If you are planning to change the way you use, design or manage your school grounds we encourage you to consider our Six Principles for Outdoor Learning and Play.

Principle One – Outdoor Learning, Play and Connection with Nature Should Be Available and Accessible for Every Child and Young Person in Every School.

Outdoor learning, play and connection with nature is an essential part of education for all. We understand that many disadvantaged children are less likely to have access to this. Our work reduces inequality by ensuring access to well-designed school grounds for all, informed by the needs, ideas and aspirations of the children and young people who will use these spaces.

Principle Two – Outdoor Learning Should Be Fully Integrated into a School's Curriculum.

Blending subject-specific knowledge with context-specific experiences in the outdoor environment supports children and young people to acquire deeper meaning, increase motivation and support their wellbeing. Our programmes support educators to deliver high-quality outdoor learning.

Principle Three – All Children and Young People Should Have Access to High-Quality Outdoor Play.

Children and young people deserve and benefit from extended periods of play during every school day. These periods of play should be a protected part of every school day.

Our programmes give children and young people opportunities to play in challenging, adventurous and enriching environments that incorporate natural elements.

Principle Four – The Natural World Should Be at the Heart of All School Grounds.

All school grounds should provide children and young people with enriching opportunities to connect with nature. Our programmes encourage them to appreciate the natural world, become stewards of the environment and protect the future health of their planet.

Principle Five – The Whole of the School Grounds Should Be an Outdoor Classroom.

All outdoor elements, including asphalt, paving, brick walls and sand pits provide space and resources for learning alongside the natural world. The entire school grounds are an outdoor classroom and no limits should be set on what is used for teaching and learning outdoors.

Principle Six – School Grounds Should Be Designed for the Future and Made to Last.

Planned changes to school grounds should engage the whole school community, consider the entire site and the multiple ways it can be used. In our programmes we encourage educators to consider the long-term use, design and management of school grounds and underpin these decisions with the United Nations Global Sustainable Development Goals.

PART 1
PRACTICALITIES

1
Taking your learning outdoors

We've identified some reasons for taking learning outdoors (see Figure 1.1). We have left some gaps for you to add your own.

PLANNING YOUR JOURNEY

In this next section we will help you plan your journey – from where you are now to where you want to be. By looking through this section and by trying out some of the activities you will discover new ideas, techniques and processes that will help you build your confidence and develop your outdoor teaching skills and knowledge. We hope that you will become someone who not only enjoys taking lessons outside but sees the benefits this can bring for your pupils.

WHERE AM I NOW?

We'd like you to feel you have built your confidence in teaching outside as you use this book, so let's start by thinking about where you are now with your practice and confidence in teaching outside.

To help you understand where you are now we suggest you look at Figure 1.2 and complete it by putting yourself on a scale of one to ten for each question. This will help you to see where you have gaps and where you might want to focus on more.

If you find yourself towards the left-hand end with low scores on more than one of these scales we hope that you will find answers and ideas in this book to help you move towards the right-hand side. Some challenges will be easier than others to address, for example we

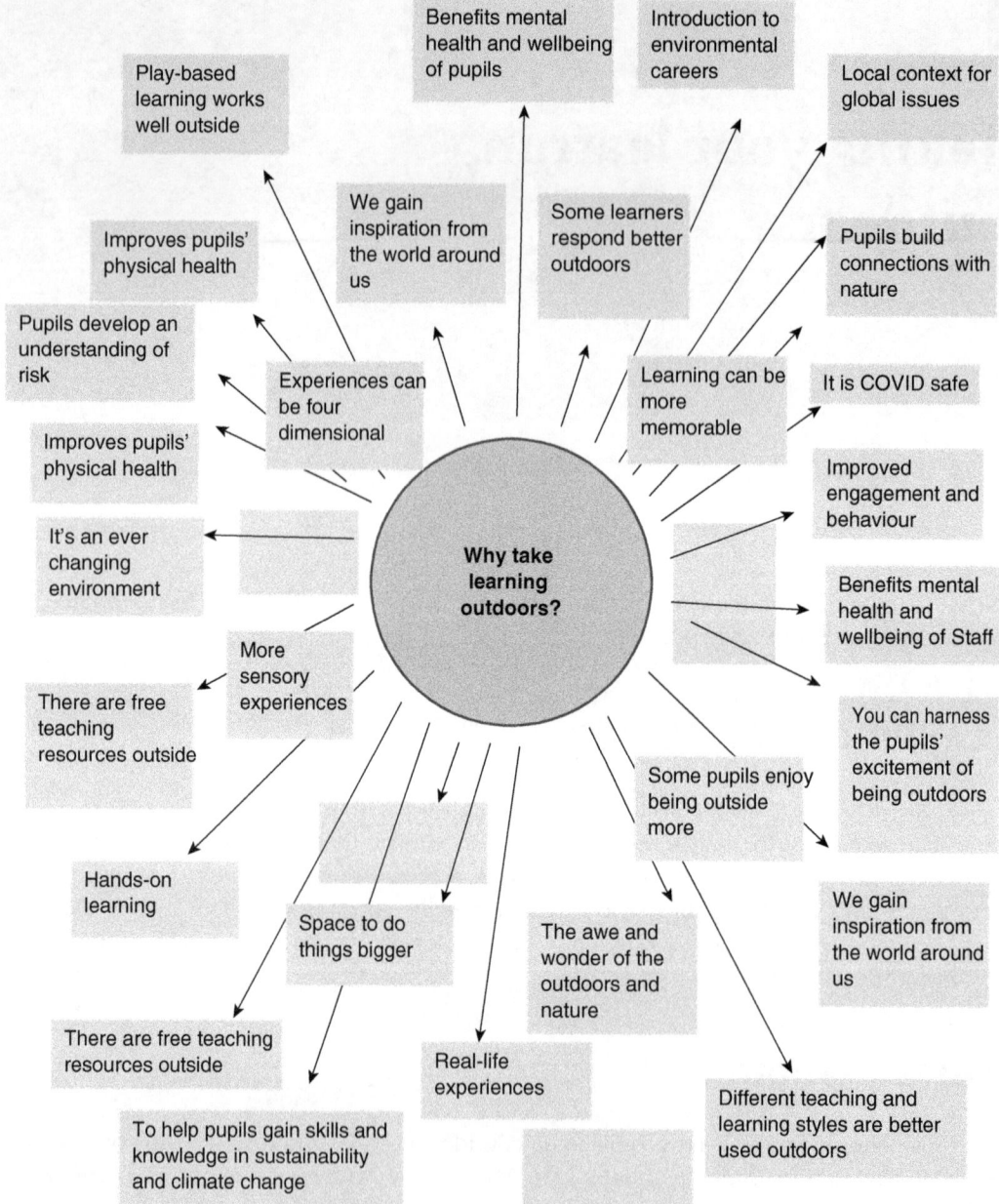

Figure 1.1

will show you ideas that don't need lots of equipment, whilst others might be harder, for example if you have a senior management team who don't believe in teaching outside. Even for this challenge we hope this book will help to convince them!

I don't teach outside now									I teach outside every day
1	2	3	4	5	6	7	8	9	10

I don't have confidence in taking my class outside									I feel confident in taking my class outside
1	2	3	4	5	6	7	8	9	10

I don't have the knowledge I need to take lessons outdoors									I have the knowledge I need to take lessons outdoors
1	2	3	4	5	6	7	8	9	10

I don't have the skills I need to take lessons outdoors									I have the skills I need to take lessons outdoors
1	2	3	4	5	6	7	8	9	10

I don't have the lesson ideas to take my class outside									I have lots of ideas for taking my class outside
1	2	3	4	5	6	7	8	9	10

I don't have the support from senior management									I have great support from senior management
1	2	3	4	5	6	7	8	9	10

I don't have the resources to teach outside									I have lots of resources to help me teach outside
1	2	3	4	5	6	7	8	9	10

I don't have the space to teach outside									I have lots of spaces in which to teach outside
1	2	3	4	5	6	7	8	9	10

Figure 1.2

WHERE DO I WANT TO BE AND HOW CAN I GET THERE?

Now we want you to really think about where you are aiming to reach, and this can be different for everyone. Do you want to take the occasional lesson outside or do you see the outdoors as a space you will take your class every day? Maybe you want to lead outdoor learning at your school? You may be new to teaching or someone with years of experience; everyone is different so everyone's journey will be different too.

Again we ask you to consider some statements to help you establish your needs so that you can then start to plan what you will need to do to reach your goal (see Figure 1.3). Start in the left-hand column and circle where you are now, then move to the right-hand column and circle where you want to be.

As you move across the page from where you are now to where you want to be, circle the actions you plan to take. The higher your aim in the right-hand column the more you will benefit from elements towards the top of the other columns. You may change your mind later as your aim changes – maybe you just want to teach a few more lessons outside now, but in a year or two, as you build your confidence, knowledge and skills, you may want to aim higher and so will need to consider other actions along the way.

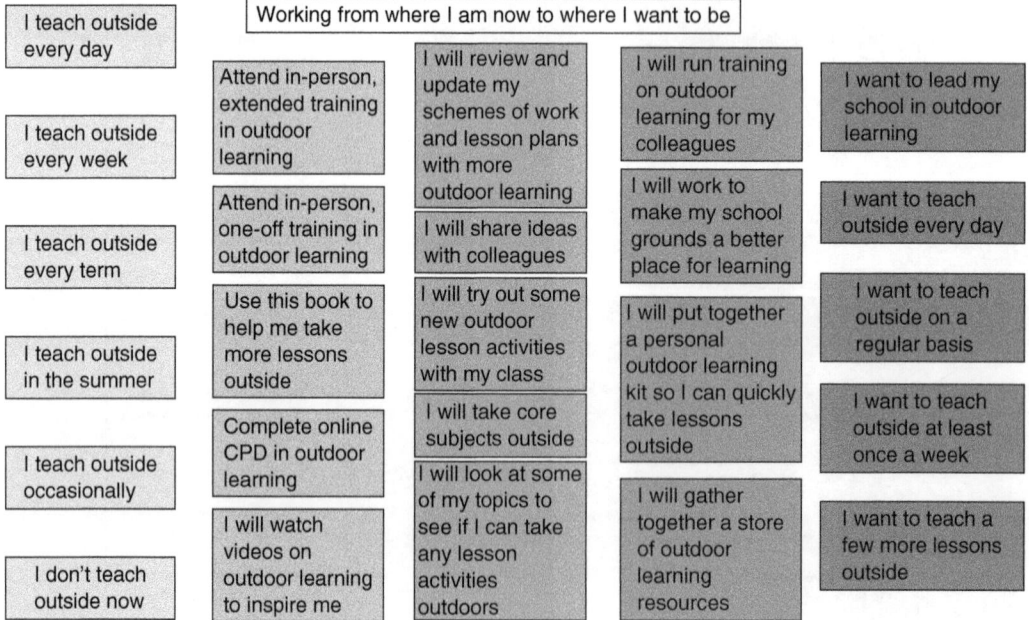

Figure 1.3

MAKING THE CHANGES

This is where you do the work – but it is down to you how you do this. Work at your own speed, take it one step at a time then look back and reflect on what you have achieved. We suggest you keep revisiting the statements in the 'Where am I now?' to check your progress along the way.

And don't forget you are modelling behaviour with how you interact with and care for the outdoor environment when you teach outside, so make sure you consider this every time you take your pupils outdoors.

2

Some inspiration from schools

PREPARING YOUR GROUNDS FOR TEACHING AND LEARNING

You can teach outside even if you have the smallest piece of asphalt or have to use a space outside of your site, but the more variety you have access to the greater the range of activities you can teach. There is an array of things that will help everyone to teach outside more easily – these include having seating and/or gathering spaces, providing shade and shelter and creating storage outdoors.

In this section we give you a few ideas of things that will make your grounds a better space to teach in. This is not the place to help you make major changes to your grounds (see our toolkit for primary schools, *Learn and Play Out*) but we can give you a few pointers to help make teaching outside a better experience for all.

Consider the statements in Table 2.1. They don't cover everything but are a good starting point for thinking about your spaces for bringing groups together. We have also given you a range of examples of how other schools have addressed the need for facilities for teaching and learning in their grounds.

We suggest you use our *school grounds audit tool* if you want to look more closely at your wider school grounds (see Chapter 17 for more information about how to get hold of a copy of the Learning through Landscape (LtL) audit tool).

Whatever changes you make to your grounds, start by thinking about what you want to *do* outside rather than what you want to *have*. When you know what *experiences* you want your pupils to have outdoors then you can work out what needs to change in order for that to happen. That may just be a change in attitude, a change in your schemes of work or changes to your grounds. If this is the case then this section will help you get started.

SOME INSPIRATION FROM SCHOOLS

Table 2.1 Thinking about seating and gathering spaces for teaching and learning

All you need is a space to bring a class together to start teaching outside but having an 'official' space to meet in can help elevate the importance of outdoor learning.

Whilst you can spend a lot of money building a substantial seating area, you can also create spaces to gather that cost much less. You might like to start with something temporary and test out alternative layouts or positions before you decide if you want a permanent feature in your grounds.

Imagine you are teaching a group outside –

- How many people will use the seating or space?
- How big are they? (adults are a very different size to children)
- Where does the seating or gathering space need to be located? Near to where you will teach, such as by the growing beds or in the wild area? Not disturbing other classes?
- How easy is it for everyone to access?
- Do we definitely want seats or should we consider other ways to bring a class together such as painted concentric circles for pupils to gather on?
- What layout will work best? - Circles and horseshoes often work well.
- Do we want something for pupils to lean on, such as a bench top, or will we always use clipboards?
- How many seating or gathering spaces do we need?
- Do we need the spaces to feel informal or formal? - what atmosphere do we want to create?
- Do we want different spaces to accommodate small and large groups?
- Can we use something to sit on that has more than one function eg a dividing wall, the edge of a planter, storage under seats or even a climbing structure with lots of levels to sit on?
- Do we want our seating to be open or enclosed with some sort of roof or temporary cover?
- Would we like something that is raised above ground level?
- Can the gathering space have a theme that can be used in other ways, such as being a round house?

Try different layouts out first, maybe take seats or mats outside, or try straw bales before deciding if you want to make a permanent feature. Moveable seats are more flexible and can accommodate wheelchairs easily and they can also be rearranged into small groups. However, they can be removed from site more easily too.

Some inspiration from schools

(Continued)

Table 2.1 (Continued)

Thinking about shade and shelter

Having shade and shelter outside will mean you can use your seating and gathering spaces throughout the year and spend more time teaching outdoors. Work through the questions below to help you decide what would work best in your school grounds.

- What way will pupils be facing as they look at staff? – try to avoid seating where they look directly into the sun or bring in shade to help.
- Do we want a temporary or permanent structure? – consider the cost against the benefits you will get from something that is fixed or something that can be moved (remember the sun moves so the shade will move too!).
- Do we have shade or shelter already from existing trees or structures? Could we think about locating the seating under these?
- Do we need shade throughout the year? Deciduous trees provide more shade in the summer when you need it most.

A pergola can form a structure over which plants can grow, creating more shade. Whilst you are waiting for this to happen, hang a sheet over the top to create shadows below.

Consider where to place seating under trees (do not place the seating around the tree trunk – this will obstruct views and prevent good interaction) so that the shade falls over the seats at the hottest time of day.

Shelter doesn't have to be permanent, especially if you don't have large amounts of money to spend. Make your money go further by considering simple options such as tarpaulins and tent-like structures or parasols with sturdy bases so they cannot be knocked over. These will also add to the shade in the grounds.

You might like to challenge pupils to build dens and then you will have shaded spaces for small groups to gather in.

Willow is another good way to make a gathering space, or to bring nature nearby – take advice on how and where to plant this and be ready to maintain it every year.

Some inspiration from schools

Thinking about storage

Having outdoor storage will make it easier for you to take more lessons outdoors as you will have equipment near to hand and won't have to carry heavy loads in and out every time you take lessons outdoors. Consider the following when planning your storage.

- What do you want to store outside? – this will help you decide what type and shape of storage you need.
- Does the storage need to be waterproof?
- Do you want your pupils to be able to access the equipment being stored?
- Do you want to keep things in one specific space or on a routeway outside?
- How secure does your storage need to be?
- Can you use walls and fences to hang things on? This can be useful if you are particularly short of space.
- Can your storage double up as something else such as a black or white board, decking or even seating?

Some inspiration from schools

3

Sustainability and climate change

As more people become aware of the importance of sustainability and the need to address climate change, so schools need to address these issues too. The average school grounds in the UK are over 2 hectares in size, meaning that across the UK school grounds cover more than 61,000 hectares of land.

School grounds are therefore key to addressing climate change and can have an impact in a number of ways:

- They can help to mitigate the impacts of both drought and flooding through changes in surfacing, mulching, water collection and drainage.
- They can help in the fight against future climate change through planting and grounds management changes.
- They can help to increase biodiversity through the addition of wildlife habitats or the way grounds are managed.
- Soils are at threat due to climate change and these can be improved through management such as incorporating home-made compost.
- Resources can be created that support teaching about sustainability and climate change such as wildlife habitats, new planting and adding shade.
- Pupils can also learn about climate change through the process of surveying, planning and developing their grounds.
- Grounds that are developed with nature in mind provide more opportunities for learning, play and connecting with nature, and regular access to natural spaces helps to develop good mental health and wellbeing in pupils and staff alike.
- School grounds can be places that bring the community together to both consider the issues of climate change and to share in the benefits of cool spaces as temperatures rise.

Towards the end of the book there is a section looking at teaching through themes rather than subject areas. One of these themes is 'Biodiversity in our school grounds', which will help you to start to address issues of sustainability and climate change in and through your school grounds.

4

Tackling the challenges and obstacles

WE JUST DON'T HAVE THE SPACE!

MAKING THE MOST OF WHAT YOU HAVE GOT

You may think it is all very well teaching outside if you have large school grounds, or ones with loads of features, but what do you do if you only have a small, dull patch of asphalt, or virtually nothing at all? Well, we believe there are some things you can do to help you make the most of what you do have, and also think about other spaces that might be available for you to use too.

First, review the spaces you have, however small. Sometime this space will have been eroded over the years as temporary classrooms move in or the car park is expanded; maybe the bins take priority over pupils or an area has become rundown and possibly even unsafe due to poor maintenance. Consider if better use can be made of these spaces by moving things around or prioritising the pupils and their right to outdoor learning and play. Look at the vertical space you have too. By that we mean look at walls, fences, hedges and upwards as well as just at the ground. These vertical spaces can be great for storage or be sites for information boards, boards for chalking on or murals and mosaics. If you are adding structures think about having different layers, for example a raised platform could have either storage or a play space under it, thus doubling the surface area you can use.

Secondly, look at timetabling the space you have. This would be the same approach as you would use with something like the school hall.

Thirdly, look at expanding the space you have by using adjoining places. You might have publicly owned land which could be requested for use during school hours. Other schools may have a private space right next to their grounds, such as a church or community hall's grounds or those belonging to a private business. As it adjoins the school it will bring minimal extra risk and no extra staff needed, so permission to use the space could be sought.

Our final point is around new schools or renovations. The right and need for children to be outdoors for learning and play is unarguable. However, you may not have much say as to where or how the site for a new school is being developed, and in particular what the outside space is like. We believe school grounds should have the same priority, thought and assets assigned to them as the school building, but sometimes school grounds can be last in the budget and even that can disappear. As with all of education, this is about the best quality of learning experience, not the minimum required by law or guidance. So, if you do get a say in the design or changes of a school, make sure that the needs of the pupils are considered so that they will have access to high-quality, nature-rich spaces in which to play and learn.

FINDING SPACE OUTSIDE THE GROUNDS

Some new schools have little, if any, school grounds to speak of, but the need for children to spend time outside is still vitally important. So how do you find ways around this? Working creatively and in partnership can lead to some great outdoor learning opportunities, but they will take some planning.

One of the most common barriers to taking learning off-site is the problem of staff ratios. However, under 'Routine and Expected' principles this is more flexible than you may think. This principle is used across the UK when considering local, routine school trips. It uses a risk–benefit approach, considering how many adults might practically be needed rather than a blanket ratio. This approach is endorsed by the Health and Safety Executive (HSE), the Outdoor Education Advisers' Panel (OEAP) and Scottish Advisory Panel for Outdoor Education (SAPOE).

If you are a school in this situation, start by taking a look at an online map in satellite view. This can highlight where local greenspaces are. Parents can also be an excellent resource here – they know the community well and can suggest places you may not have considered. Possible sites include parks, hotel grounds, business parks, 'stalled spaces' with no apparent owner, council office gardens, and other local schools or colleges.

In our experience, businesses or landowners often welcome schools as part of their community and social responsibility schemes and this can help to build good school–community relationships. It can also be a good literacy exercise to get a class to write to a landowner, explaining why they would like to use the space.

GOING OUTSIDE WHATEVER THE WEATHER?

The weather is often cited as a barrier to learning outdoors, but the changing weather through the seasons provides a rich, real-world learning resource that can also help to support a healthy immune system. Whilst the rain may be the first thing you think of that might make you think twice about going outside, really hot, sunny days can be a challenge too. Do always check on the forecast ahead of time and don't go out if it is going to be very windy or a storm is brewing. Safety must obviously come first.

If children and staff are going to access the school grounds whatever the weather, then appropriate clothing is essential. It is important to develop and communicate your wet weather policy with parents and a store of spare clothes can be used to support those pupils who still come ill-equipped. Consider requesting donations from siblings, use of unclaimed clothing in lost property and a dedicated fundraiser to help promote positive practice.

The right equipment matters too. Use a cover for a clipboard and pencils rather than pens when you take pupils out as these will continue to work if it starts to rain.

Including a form of covered space outdoors ensures that children can seek shelter on wet days and shade on sunny days. A tarpaulin provides a low cost, easy to store shelter solution that can be erected and dismantled quickly and provides the flexibility of use in a variety of spaces and locations. A more permanent alternative could be erected as funding allows.

Ice and snow bring their own challenges, but also provide exciting learning opportunities and a chance for children to learn how to modify their behaviour in order to negotiate the associated experiences (for example walking over ice on the ground).

There are, of course, a wide range of curriculum links associated with the weather – from the use of different instruments to measure wind, rainfall and temperature to identifying the best location for outdoor seating or the creation of an area to support wildlife.

It is worth noting that when given the choice, pupils will regularly choose to go outside during wet break and lunchtimes, which can have a positive impact on their behaviour in subsequent lessons. However, the enjoyment and learning outcomes will be limited if pupils are forced to go outdoors to learn in particularly inclement weather.

WHAT EQUIPMENT DO WE NEED?

Sourcing equipment to take your learning outdoors can be seen as a barrier when budgets are tight within settings, but it doesn't need to be expensive. Even without any additional resources, you can still go outside and teach brilliant lessons, so don't let it stop you. Keep it simple – natural resources such as sticks and leaves can be used for a huge number of activities and are free!

Try looking at what kit you already have in school: you will be surprised at what is currently unused but would be great for your outdoor supplies. Ask local companies and your parent community for any donations of specific items – this could even be a persuasive letter-writing activity for the older children.

The main essential is that your pupils have appropriate clothing and shelter, if needed, and remember your first aid kit and emergency supplies if you are venturing further away from the school building.

Below is a list of useful items for a range of outdoor curriculum experiences. Start with a small selection and build on this as your practice develops. We have provided a checklist (see Figure 4.1) but do add your own ideas as you put your kit together.

FOR WRITING OR RECORDING

- clipboards (can be made using card and a peg/elastic band/bulldog clip);
- scrap card/paper;
- white board and pens;
- pencils (will work in all weathers!);
- chalk.

TRANSPORTING AND COLLECTING

- containers – old egg boxes or plastic packaging works well;
- funnels and jugs;
- sieves and colanders.

NATURAL MATERIALS

- sticks;
- leaves;
- pebbles/stones;
- wooden discs;
- pine cones/conkers.

ACTIVITY SPECIFIC (SEE ALSO EQUIPMENT FOR EACH ACTIVITY)

- tarpaulins or old sheets;
- rope/twine/string;
- blindfolds;
- tape measures/rulers;
- colour palettes – great for scavenger hunts.

Everyday kit – some examples are given below but make your own list for different activities

○ Containers to collect things in   ○ Clipboards – shop bought or homemade

○ Scrap card or paper   ○ Pencils

○ Chalk   ○ White boards and pens

○   ○

Specialist kit – some examples are given below but make your own list for different activities

○ Tarpaulins or old sheets   ○ Blindfolds

○ Tape measures   ○ Rope/twine/string/strips

○   ○

○   ○

Figure 4.1

MANAGING RISK AND CHALLENGE IN SCHOOL GROUNDS

Risk is a natural part of daily life. It can never be removed entirely from anything we do, so it is important that, as children grow up, we teach them to deal with risk. We do this as we teach them to cross the road, carry scissors safely or take a science lesson outside. In this way they will be able to make considered decisions when they face new risks in the future. Learning to assess and deal with risks is an important part of your pupils' education and development, and outdoor learning can support the progress of these vital skills.

Children gain a range of benefits from being challenged and facing risky situations: they learn and experience an emotional response to failure and success, they learn to judge where to be careful and what is a reasonable level of fear, and they gain enjoyment from the triumph of success in meeting a challenge.

Whatever approach and decisions you make, the pupils should 'see' the process. At a simple level this may be asking them about their concerns and how they could mitigate, or even if they need to mitigate, those risks. It is not a substitute for your preparation and judgement, but is a vital element in teaching children about making risk judgements.

SO HOW DO WE GET THE BALANCE RIGHT?

Teachers should expect their schools to have procedures that encourage participation in learning activities and are proportionate to the level of risk. In relation to school grounds this means no additional paperwork or permissions beyond the following:

- An annual risk assessment and simple control measures for the school grounds. This is no different to the indoor classroom.
- A simple inspection routine for the grounds that will help maintain a rich learning and play environment.
- A staff team who have access to risk assessments, and the simple protocols they are expected to work within.
- Clarity on who is responsible for the three above points.

Please note that 'Routine and Expected' local trips also only require an annual permission and annual risk assessment, and both these can be generic for such things as 'visiting a park' or 'museum visit'.

In order to get this balance right we encourage schools to use a risk–benefit approach when evaluating their grounds (see Figure 4.2). At its simplest this means that when you consider a space you want to use or review an activity you want to run, you look at the benefits pupils will gain alongside the risks and make a judgement about how these two factors balance out.

A good example of acceptable and reasonable risk-taking would be learning to run – an activity we would all encourage and accept without question. You would not ban running because of one fall on sports day or in the playground. Furthermore, we would expect staff to make reasonable judgements around this – on sports day you support running faster, in the school corridor you advocate walking.

PUTTING THIS INTO PRACTICE

Whilst you can create a risk–benefit approach from scratch you can also adapt your established risk-assessment systems to include the evaluation of the benefits gained from using a place or from an activity.

Follow this pathway and you will start to see if the activities you undertake outside balance benefit with risk. This balance isn't about a numerical calculation. It is up to you to judge if the level of benefit is greater than the level of allowable risk.

It is important that you focus on the level of harm that might occur from an accident. A minor slip or tumble on grass would not appear on a risk assessment. Falling off an item of play equipment high enough to cause a significant injury would. The UK Health and Safety Executive identifies which injuries are reportable and which are not; this gives an indication of what level of harm they consider to be serious. For example, a broken limb is reportable but a broken finger or thumb is not. See their 'Types of reportable incidents' to clarify these different levels of harm.

Do bear in mind that many benefits are longer term, whereas many risks can be immediate, and that there can be multiple risks and benefits. In our 'running' example, colliding in a corridor is very immediate, but long-term benefits of running include increased physical literacy, improved health and wellbeing and possible future careers or pastimes.

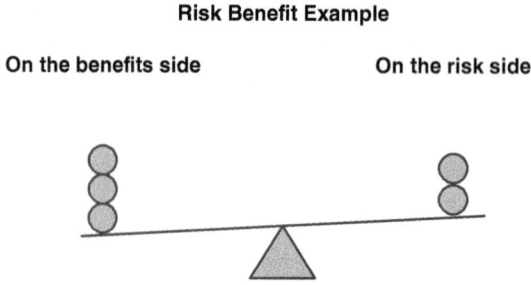

Figure 4.2

You will also make risk–benefit judgements as you work with the children – this is your dynamic risk assessment. In our 'running' example, you would already know when to ask pupils to walk (in the corridor) and when to encourage them to run as fast as they can on sports day.

DEVELOPING A CULTURE AROUND RISK

Risk is a subject that every colleague and parent will have a view about, and every person's judgement around risk will vary. There are, therefore, standardised procedures for managing risk in every school – your existing risk management system. It is important that you work with them to keep within a normality of risk, but are able to challenge them when some are myths or overly cautious. You should always refer back to the paperwork and what precedents exist elsewhere.

TACKLING THE CHALLENGES AND OBSTACLES

Your culture and judgements around risk management also need communicating with colleagues and parents. At Learning through Landscapes (LtL) we do this by publishing our risk management documents on our website.

(See Chapter 17 for further reading on risk.)

WHAT ABOUT POLLUTION PROBLEMS?

One of the reasons you may head outdoors with your pupils is to find 'fresh air'. However, it is a reality that for many schools close to roads or other sources of pollution, air quality can be quite poor and should be checked regularly. The simplest way of monitoring air quality is through a free app. Our staff have used IQAirQuality in many countries and found it reliable. The level at which your school decides not to be outdoors is a decision that you have to make. Typically we advise caution at levels over 100 on the US Air Quality Index (US AQI).

One key thing to remember is that air quality can change over surprisingly short distances. Shrubs and trees have (varying) ability to both absorb pollutants and deposit pollutants from the air onto their own leaves or nearby surfaces due to transpiration activity, so if you have plants between the pollution and the space you are using this can make a difference.

Looking at air quality is not only valuable for your health and that of your pupils, it is also something they can study. Check to see if there are local, national or international programmes for schools you can take part in. They may provide information and resources to help you study the pollution in your grounds and discover how this relates to pollution in both nearby schools and those in other locations.

Pollution is also a key climate change issue and pupils may want to find out more about both local and international polluters. They might decide to take action by writing letters, designing posters or adding some planting to their grounds and measuring the impact this has.

BUT I HAVE TO TEACH THE CURRICULUM

Teachers are sometimes concerned that outdoor learning might not be 'real' learning. Or they have a list of things they have to teach and limited time in which to do it and feel that going outside might not allow them to get this completed. Well, we hope that this book will show you that teaching outdoors can be just as effective as teaching the curriculum inside, and for some topics, even better.

At LtL we frequently see children who struggle inside thriving outdoors in an environment that suits them better, whilst more able pupils are stretched by practical, problem-solving activities in ways that are different from the techniques they use indoors. Complex concepts can come alive as hands-on learning using physical representations or real-life examples help clarify and reinforce ideas and understanding, whilst just being in a different space can also help to make learning stick.

Sometimes we must trust that the practical learning we are doing outside will be shown in later follow-up work, where their understanding of a concept will be demonstrated. Outdoor activities can also be used as a stimulus or lead into higher-quality outputs in the lesson that follows, such as a piece of writing or the use of outdoor findings as data in maths.

You may worry that teaching your curriculum lessons outside can make it difficult to evidence the learning that's taking place. There may naturally be less work in pupils' books, but this does not mean that they haven't been learning! Make sure your school leaders support and understand this, so they are not necessarily expecting written outcomes from every lesson.

It can help to think about the early years model of sharing learning through observations and other forms of less formal evidence. Pictures can be taken of lesson activities, or speech bubbles/post-it notes written quickly by your pupils to explain what they learnt outside.

Think about the outdoors when you are completing longer-term planning and look for opportunities to take the learning outside. Some simple changes to an activity can turn it from an indoor to an outdoor lesson and may require less preparation or formal marking. You could even start by simply taking an activity outside that you had planned for inside, such as guided reading or a drama lesson. This will still have lots of benefits for both pupils and staff.

STAYING IN CONTROL AND MANAGING BEHAVIOUR

Managing pupil behaviour in an outdoor setting can be out of our comfort zone for some and can feel more daunting than when we are inside a classroom. However, our perceptions are often proved wrong, and some children will respond better and be more engaged with learning outside.

Behaviour management starts in the classroom, ensuring your pupils are prepared to go outside and have been given clear expectations for the session.

If, currently, their outdoor experiences at school are rare, then of course it will be a novelty and there will be excitement about going out. Give them time initially to release some excitement and get ready to learn. Remember, the more routine their outdoor experiences are, the more they will get used to it and your grounds will just become another place that they learn.

Introduce outdoor learning gradually so that both you and your pupils familiarise yourselves with new routines. You do not have to spend your entire lesson outside – perhaps begin with just the starter of your session, or a small section of the day such as a reading activity, a mental maths game or collecting vocabulary or data for use in a lesson.

Freedom of movement and exploration is a key benefit to being outside, so ensure you set clear boundaries of where your pupils can go and have a way to bring them back to a base or central location such as a bespoke call, duck whistle, bell, tambourine, etc.

Bear in mind that there can be a variety of factors that will affect behaviour and you will likely see totally different actions outside compared to inside. You will see changes to individual pupils; for example some may have a fear of getting dirty, struggle with the potential sensory overload or hold negative connotations with outside due to previous encounters or even playtime experiences. Communicating with parents can further help the children to prepare and may also inform you of any potential behaviour problems you might encounter.

BUT I JUST DON'T HAVE THE TIME!

The bonus of teaching your curriculum outside is that it can be as simple as moving the location of your lesson, rather than it being an additional subject to cover.

Getting ready to go outside may take longer initially but once the children build up a routine and practice a few times, they will get quicker at it. Older children can be tasked with getting changed at break or lunchtime, so they are ready to go at the start of the lesson.

Another time saver is to link your outdoor learning time to when the children are already outside or about to go outdoors, such as straight after or before breaktime, before or after lunch or at the end of the day. Simply meet them out there, do your activity, then head back in, cutting out one of the transition times. Or, at the other end of the lesson, finish outside. If younger children require snacks in the middle of a lesson, allow them to eat these outside as part of the activity so you are reducing how often you move location.

Look around your school site for the most accessible spaces. It is likely each class has quicker access to a certain area that can be used for shorter parts of lessons. It does not have to be a full lesson every time, or the most natural, open space either – just a small courtyard out the back of a classroom can provide an area for an outdoor experience.

Lastly, save time by having any equipment ready to go in grab bags or clearly stored in areas that are accessible for the children. This can include having storage space outside. The faster it is to get the kit and put it away again, the more time you have to enjoy the outdoors.

5
Accessibility and inclusion

All children, whatever their abilities, strengths and interests, should be able to access outdoor learning. This does not mean every child will be able to access every learning activity we have provided in the same way, but they can all take part in outdoor learning in a positive way.

Inclusion in outdoor learning is about looking at how everyone in your class can be involved together, all gaining from the activities they are taking part in. Consider the sensory elements of the activity, your pupils' academic and physical abilities, the interaction of pupils with each other and the overall experiences gained. All children are different and will be engaged and enthused by different things, and all teachers are familiar with creating lessons that meet these different needs so that all their pupils can flourish. Teaching outdoors is no different.

Think about how you can make your outdoor learning accessible to all your pupils. When considering the physical accessibility of your site look at the following:

- Find or create routes and pathways around your grounds that enable everyone to reach different parts of your site.
- Think about the sensory aspects of your grounds – sensory overload can be difficult for some pupils to cope with, so review the way different senses are stimulated across your grounds.
- Consider the visual clues around the site, from signage to contrasting colours used in different areas or alongside pathways.
- Examine the auditory aspects of your grounds – does sound echo between buildings and hard surfaces? Will different groups disturb each other, inside and out?
- Challenge should be offered to all in different ways, such as using deliberately bumpy pathway surfaces or obstacles to move around for wheelchair users. Think about the degree of challenge within each activity.

- Think about the layout and structure of seating and gathering spaces to ensure all can join in learning together.
- Consider the equipment you use and whether it needs adapting for different pupils.

In addition, consider each activity you use outside to make sure that all your pupils can be properly included. How will each pupil access the learning? Will everyone be able to be included in an active way and not just be an observer? Think about how you can adapt each activity to the needs of your class, whether that is by considering how each pupil can take an active role in a task, by changing the way they retrieve information or how they gather and record the information collected or created. And don't forget this also means thinking about how you stretch your pupils too.

6
Making it last

Sustaining your outdoor learning practice and ensuring it remains a key part of your setting can be a challenge. It is important to maintain enthusiasm and engagement in it even after an initial investment changes or when the weather turns!

It is vital that teaching outdoors is part of your whole school ethos, and everyone has a responsibility and commitment to it. This prevents a breakdown in action when a key person leaves your setting or changes role. It should be an integral part of how you teach across the school, regardless of year group or staff personal preference. Ultimately, you want outdoor learning to become a habit, so plan carefully how you can remove any barriers and make it as easy as possible for all staff to achieve it.

Celebrate the learning that is taking place and raise its profile across the school by sharing displays, photos or even having an outdoor learner of the week award alongside your other prizes. Regularly communicate your progress with parents and the wider school community to further celebrate successes or to ask for support and volunteers.

In a practical sense, make sure you have an inventory of equipment and have a system in place if items get damaged. If you can buy resources, try to invest in good quality items such as waterproofs that will last and save money for replacements down the line. Make sure the school-site team are on board, know what the benefits are of using the grounds more for learning and are aware of what you are trying to achieve. This will help you to create and continue to develop a rich environment to teach your curriculum in.

For the longer term, include outdoor learning in your school improvement plan, creating goals and aims to maintain and continually develop your provision. Referring to the LtL Six Principles of Outdoor Learning and Play will help you do this. Make sure schemes of work and lesson plans are regularly reviewed to establish if elements can be taken outside and share this amongst the staff. Set aside staff meeting time and regular continuing professional development (CPD) sessions to increase confidence and share ideas or concerns across the team. These could include regular reviews of what you have achieved on your outdoor learning journey and what you want to develop next. The key to making it last is having engaged, confident and well-trained staff, so make the time to invest in this.

7
Myth busting

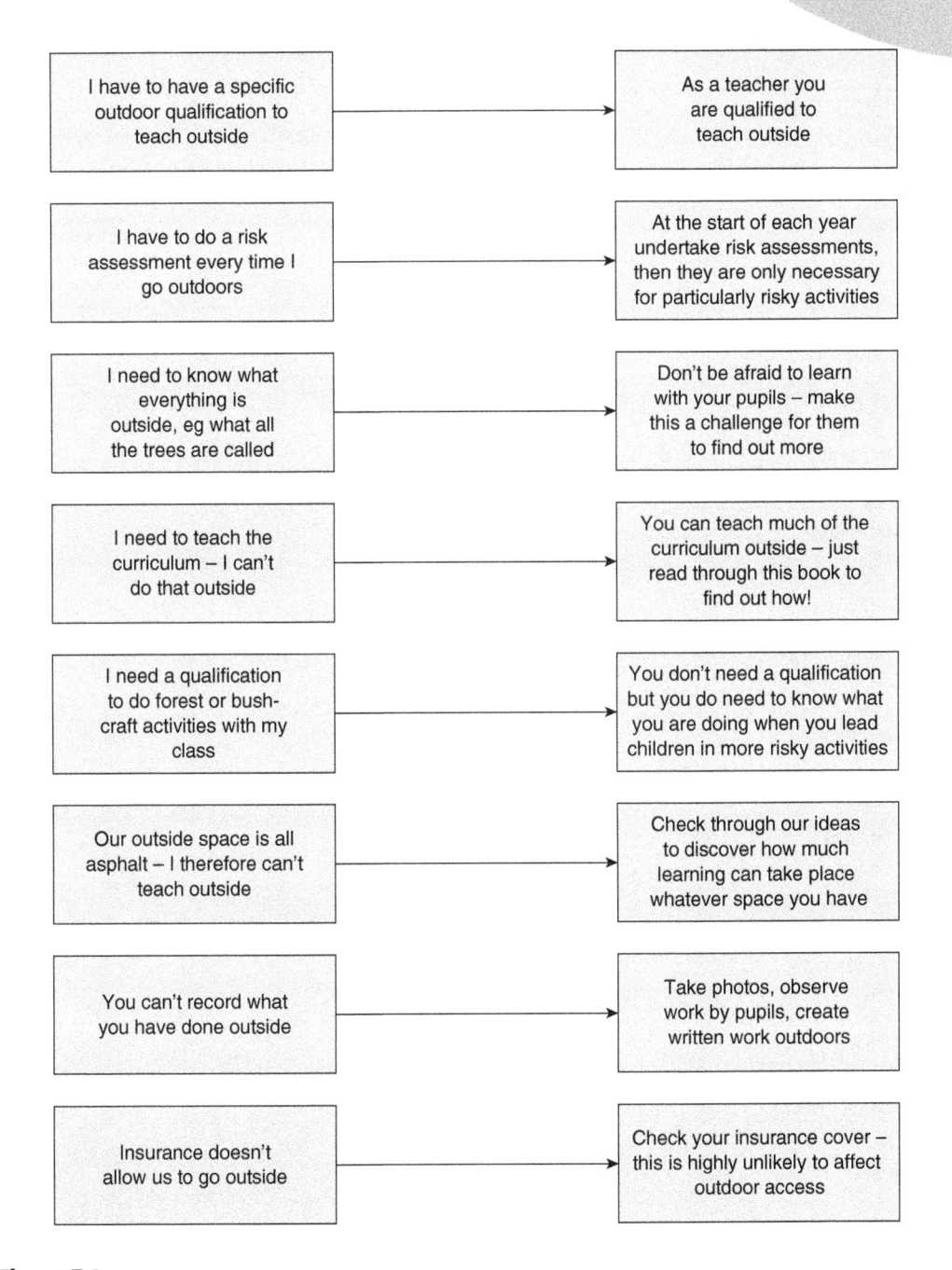

Myth	Reality
I have to have a specific outdoor qualification to teach outside	As a teacher you are qualified to teach outside
I have to do a risk assessment every time I go outdoors	At the start of each year undertake risk assessments, then they are only necessary for particularly risky activities
I need to know what everything is outside, eg what all the trees are called	Don't be afraid to learn with your pupils – make this a challenge for them to find out more
I need to teach the curriculum – I can't do that outside	You can teach much of the curriculum outside – just read through this book to find out how!
I need a qualification to do forest or bush-craft activities with my class	You don't need a qualification but you do need to know what you are doing when you lead children in more risky activities
Our outside space is all asphalt – I therefore can't teach outside	Check through our ideas to discover how much learning can take place whatever space you have
You can't record what you have done outside	Take photos, observe work by pupils, create written work outdoors
Insurance doesn't allow us to go outside	Check your insurance cover – this is highly unlikely to affect outdoor access

Figure 7.1

8
Making plans

As you plan your journey, make note of what you aim to achieve over the next couple of years.

	1st term	2nd term	3rd term	Anything new in the 2nd year
Quick and easy/ warm ups etc				
Language and literacy				
Maths and numeracy				
Science				
Humanities				
The arts				
Technology and cooking				
Themes				

Figure 8.1

PART 2
ACTIVITIES FOR CURRICULUM TEACHING

● ABOUT THE ACTIVITIES

We have written this book for teachers in different nations, so we have not matched the activities to any one curriculum. We have instead chosen themes and topics that are common across nations so that we know they will fit your needs wherever you are.

In a similar way, we have not told you exactly what age an activity is for. We have given some guidance, however, by assigning low, medium or high to each activity. This is to give you an indication about how each activity fits within a progression of learning. So it is more about where your pupils are now rather than how old they are. If you are just starting out on a topic, a low-level activity might be best for your class. if you want to challenge your group more then a high-level activity could be the one for you. Sometimes we have given you three activities together that progress from one to the other. These might be used by one class or across year groups as pupils progress their learning on a particular topic.

We have added in progressions and extensions to help you think about what you could do next or to push more able pupils. In a similar way, adaptations help you consider different ways to run the same activity. These might show you how you can adapt the activity for your grounds or for specific pupils in your class.

As well as the main activities we have suggested cross-curriculum themes you could use. These are written in more of an outline form, with no set levels and with more input needed from you to make them work for your class. We have included these as inspiration and to help you plan how you might work across a year group or the whole school as well as with your individual class.

We also believe that teachers know how to teach – and, importantly, how to teach the pupils in their class, and we know how different that can be from year to year! So we want you to adapt and change these activities to fit your needs and the needs of your pupils. We have given you ideas for progression and adaptation but we expect you to change these activities even more and make them your own. We then hope you will come up with your own ideas, maybe using a method of delivery from one activity for a completely different topic or curriculum area. Enjoy changing our ideas, building on them with new ideas and coming up with something completely different as you gain your confidence outdoors.

So why not get out and get going?!

9
Language and literacy

INTRODUCING LANGUAGE AND LITERACY OUTDOORS

The natural world and your school grounds are a brilliant setting and inspiration for writing, ideas generation, discussions and explanations. Nature can be a real-life stimulus for all genres of writing, from recounts about outdoor experiences, non-fiction texts about what can be found outside and activities around environmental issues, to creative writing such as stories or poetry inspired by outdoor areas. Examples of these could be instructions about how to make a bug hotel, a non-chronological report about the tree species in the grounds, persuasive writing about why we should protect natural spaces and pollinator friendly plants or simply stories set in woodlands.

Your school grounds are also a special place for texts to come alive, settings to be explored and all levels of reading to take place. Taking your characters or storylines out of the classroom can help pupils to visualise them more clearly and develop their own creative writing skills. In addition, outdoor spaces provide natural resources that can be used to provoke the use of new vocabulary or to create story maps or characters.

The extra space provided by the playground or outdoor areas can also allow different surfaces for practising letter formation, trying out spellings or playing active games to support grammar learning. These could range from setting up obstacles to negotiate (to reinforce prepositions – through, under, over, etc.) or 'corners' to explore different word classes (for example pupils run to different spaces depending on whether a given word is a noun, verb, adjective or adverb).

To take your literacy outside, items such as chalk, clipboards, pencils and surfaces for mark-making will be useful, generic resources that you will see featured in many of the suggested activities.

Following and listening to clues

Subject area: Language and literacy

Key focus: Listening and contributing to a discussion

Also
- teamwork and communication
- understanding and following instructions

Level: Low

Previous learning required:

To have taken part in a tour of the school grounds or general area being used, so that pupils will have an awareness of where they are being led to.

Aim of the activity:

To listen carefully to clues given and use the information to find locations and hidden items around the school grounds.

Equipment:

- large area with different locations where items can be hidden;
- clues/descriptions for you to read and share with the pupils;
- items that can be hidden at the locations for the pupils to find (see suggestions below).

Description of the activity:

The main aim of this activity is for the pupils to listen to and follow your clues, therefore the outcome of the clue and what they find at the location can be adapted to match your curriculum objectives or linked to other topics you are covering at the time. Each new clue could be found at the location described so you continue to move around the grounds as a group, or the children could be given a clue, sent to find the item and either bring it back to you at a central location or simply photograph it in its location.

Here are some suggestions of items to hide around your school site for them to find at given locations:

- sections/jigsaw pieces of a picture that can be put together, for example a story setting or character picture;
- pieces of equipment such as loose parts or craft items that they need in order to build or make something once they have all the parts;
- letters or words that will spell out a key word or a final sentence to provide a clue once they have all been found;
- natural items that can be found around the site;
- numbers that pupils must put in order or use for a further maths activity;
- shapes to be collected or described;
- written adjectives that describe a location or object, or new vocabulary that can be used for follow-up activities;
- things of a certain colour or texture;

Progression and extensions:

Challenge the children to create and share clues for each other in groups or pairs. Discuss the key information that they will need to give each other and how to make a clear description so that their clues succeed.

Adaptations:

For those children who may need additional support, pictures could be used to help show what they are looking for or the area to go to; that is photos of the location, specific plants or mini beasts to find.

A scavenger hunt activity could also be adapted to use other senses, for example give pupils an item to feel before going to find it, or play them a sound clue instead.

Circle debate

Subject area: Language and literacy

Key focus: Listening and contributing to a discussion

Also
- telling fact from fiction
- seeing things from someone else's viewpoint
- developing a persuasive line of reasoning

Level: High

Previous learning required:

To have taken part in discussions and gathering information about a topic.

Aim of the activity:

To gather information about a topic by research and listening to another person and to share information gathered.

Equipment:

- clipboards and pencils or whiteboards and markers;
- information sheets for each side of the debate.

Description of the activity:

Choose a controversial topic – one where there are two clear sides of the debate. Divide the class into two equal groups and provide your pupils with information for their side of the debate.

Here are some suggestions with some starting points for discussion:

- Building a sports centre on part of your school grounds
    - The land might not be very good and isn't used much. We have loads of field/playground already. This would give us, and the local community, better sports facilities. It would make our school more popular.
    - Once this land is changed it can never be changed back. If you build on the field then you will be removing wildlife habitats and increasing the hard surfacing, therefore helping to lead to more climate change. The money could be spent on a wider variety of things.
- We should have more lessons outside
    - Outside there is more fresh air, sunshine and nature – all of these are good for our health. We can make more noise and move around more outside. We can learn about things in practical ways and try things out for real/collect real data from outdoors.
    - It takes time to go outside, therefore we don't spend as much time learning. We don't take exams outside so why do we want to take lessons outside? Learning outdoors doesn't matter as much.

Being outside for the debate allows pupils to understand the context of the topic they are talking about, and as half the class will be talking at the same time, being outside means this is less likely to disturb other classes. The space outside also means you don't need to rearrange furniture to make space for the debate to take place.

Working with others on the same side of the debate as themselves, pupils can practise their argument, adding their own ideas to what they have been given. They can make notes to help them as they present their point of view.

Then pupils supporting one side of the argument should stand in a circle facing out and those arguing against them stand opposite them in a circle facing in.

The pupils on one side are given two minutes to present their argument to the person opposite them; then the opposing group does the same. When everyone has presented their point of view the outside group moves left by one person and the debates are repeated. Do this again so that everyone hears the opposite side of the argument three times. Each person can make notes about the opposing person's point of view.

When the group has moved around to their fourth person they have to change the side of the debate they are on, using the information they have heard from the first three people. This really makes them think about both sides of the argument and enables them to articulate another point of view.

Progression and extensions:

Instead of providing the information for the debate they can research their arguments from scratch.

Adaptations:

Allow pupils to record or take notes of the arguments they are listening to, then take these away and work with others on their side of the debate before presenting them to someone else.

Story stones

Subject area: Literacy

Key focus: To listen and identify key parts of a story

Also
- planning and editing a story

Level: Low

Previous learning required:

Knowing what is meant by terms such as characters, settings and events in relation to a fiction story.

Aim of the activity:

To follow the journey and key points of a story and inspire a love of storytelling.

Equipment:

- smooth pebbles or wooden discs;
- sharpies/marker pens;
- string;
- a familiar story;
- other natural materials that lend themselves to the story, e.g. straw and sticks for 'The Three Little Pigs'.

Description of the activity:

Collect the equipment above by asking the children to forage for pebbles, sticks and straw as part of the activity (depending on what your outside space offers). Lay out the string in a horizontal line and ask the children to sit or stand so that they can see you and the line of string.

Begin reading or telling your story. When the first characters are introduced, pupils draw these on pebbles and place them at the start of the piece of string. As the story develops, ask the children to raise their hands when you reach an important part of the tale and discuss how to represent these using words or drawings on the stones, for example the setting, key events, emotions of the characters or the ending. At each point your pupils add stones to the story, make sure everyone has something to contribute. Once you have finished telling the story, ask the class to retell it by following along the string and using the stones to help them remember the key parts. Ask if they are happy that they have covered all the most important bits of the story or if they think any more points need to be added. Explain that these stones are exactly like a plan for a story, where just the bare storyline is plotted out and put into an order.

Progression and extensions:

Invite the children to make up their own stories or create story stones for the other favourite stories that they know. Each time, encourage them to think about the key features that will help them to retell the story and share the main characters and plot to their friends.

Another way of developing the activity is to ask the children to add to or adapt the example you have created together. This could include retelling the story as they go, changing one of the stones, such as a key event or character, or making up an alternative ending.

Adaptations:

As well as pebbles, using other easily found natural materials such as wooden discs, leaves or sticks, helps to creatively represent the story's setting, and make easy links to art and design.

You can also start with some or all of the points of a story ready at the start so that your pupils work out where these should be located along the storyline, maybe adding additional ideas along the way.

The ability of your children will determine whether your story stones are mostly made up of written sentences, or pictures and symbols. By adding story stones with *openers*, for example, 'once upon a time', *conjunctions*, such as 'however' and *closing sentences* such as 'they lived happily ever after', can help children transition from verbal recounts to writing down their stories. A mixture of both pictures and written vocabulary will help children of all abilities to progress.

Leaf descriptions

Subject area: Language and literacy

Key focus: Effectively using descriptive language

Also
- understanding different word classes and the use of adjectives
- developing observational skills through using our different senses

Level: Medium

Previous learning required:

Understanding that an adjective is any word that describes a noun (an object).

Aim of the activity:

To use natural items and our senses to develop vocabulary.

Equipment:

- a leaf that can be collected by the children in the grounds of your setting (this can be one leaf per person or per group; if there are limited leaves available, these could also be collected off site and brought in);
- clipboards and pencils or whiteboards and markers.

Description of the activity:

Allow each pupil to collect a leaf from around the grounds and bring it back to the meeting point. In pairs or small groups, ask the children to begin to describe their leaves to each other and think about what the leaf looks like, feels like, smells like and even sounds like. Discuss why we will not be using our taste for this activity!

Make sure each group has access to a way of recording their ideas, e.g. a clipboard or whiteboard, and give a limited time to write down as many adjectives as they can to describe their leaves (two or three minutes).

Once the time is up, explain that you are going to play a game with these words. Each team must share one of their adjectives, taking it in turns around the groups. Explain that they need to listen carefully to each other's words, as if they repeat an adjective that has already been said, they will be out of the game. As groups are eliminated, they can become your 'ears' and listen out for any repeated words. The last group to still have new adjectives to share is the winner.

The benefit of this game is that your pupils have to listen to the adjectives provided by the other groups, meaning that they can share and magpie ideas. They are more likely to test out more complex words, as they are in a less formal setting than the classroom. The groups will also naturally discuss a wider range of descriptive words as they can explore the actual item with their different senses and physically experience it.

Progression and extensions:

The sets of adjectives that your pupils collate can then be used as a word bank that is taken back into the classroom. This can then be kept on desks to support descriptive writing, poetry or other writing projects.

Adaptations:

The same game and activity could be used for any natural item that can be found or observed in your grounds. For example, you could use sticks, flowers, clouds, rain or natural sounds.

Find a tree

Subject area: Language and literacy

Key focus: Reviewing and editing key language

Also
- choosing specific language to communicate messages effectively
- adapting and reviewing words used to ensure success

Level: Medium

Previous learning required:

Understanding that an adjective is any word that describes a noun (an object).
 Knowing that by choosing particular words we can be more effective in communicating our key message.

Aim of the activity:

To use specific adjectives to locate a particular tree.

Equipment:

- available trees or other natural objects;
- clipboards and pencils or whiteboards and markers.

Description of the activity:

Ask the children to work in pairs for this activity and give each pair a way of writing their ideas down. Explain that they are each going to choose a tree which they would like to describe, and their partner must then guess which one they picked.

Ask one of each pair to cover their eyes or turn away, so they can't see which tree their partner is choosing. Ask the other pupils to write down five words to describe their chosen tree and, without allowing much time, share these with their partner so they can locate the tree. Due to the lack of time and instruction, your pupils will probably have listed quite generic vocabulary such as green, tall, bushy, brown, etc., making it difficult for their partners to distinguish exactly which tree they were describing.

Now give them additional time to use their senses to thoroughly explore their tree and investigate carefully what it looks, feels and smells like up close.

Repeat the activity, encouraging them to think about what specific language will help communicate effectively to their partner the exact tree they are aiming to describe.

Discuss the difference between the two attempts and what made the activity more successful for them. Encourage pupils to evaluate how they could improve or edit their descriptions to increase chances of a correct guess. Explain that we do that in our writing all the time – we choose one word initially but then go back and review it to make sure we are communicating exactly what we want to our audience. Make sure you swap the partners over so that everyone has a chance at both roles.

Progression and extensions:

For more able children, progress to using descriptive sentences rather than single words. To extend learning, remove one of the pupil's senses, for example sight, so all the words used have to describe things that can be heard or felt instead of seen. This will help your pupils to categorise their words and think about what senses they refer to most when describing something.

Adaptations:

If there are limited trees in the school grounds, this activity could be completed off site in a safe and suitable area. The same game and activity could be used for a range of natural items, for example other plants, locations, sticks or leaves. Less able children could be given items to feel or look at, that they then have to match with similar items.

Create a game

Subject area: Language and literacy

Key focus: Providing clear written instructions

Also
- understanding that instructions need to follow a sequence from start to finish
- developing imagination by fitting ideas into a framework

Level: High

Previous learning required:

It would be helpful to start this activity by playing a few traditional games such as hopscotch, skipping or tag to remind pupils about the structure of instructions for games.

Aim of the activity:

To create a set of instructions for a new outdoor game.

Equipment:

- items to use in the game, for example skipping ropes, flower pots, boxes and tubes, chalk and small tokens (such as pebbles), or any other PE equipment or recycled items for use in the games your pupils create;
- clipboards, paper and pencils or whiteboards and markers;
- pre-printed sheets of prompts (see below for examples).

Description of the activity:

Begin by reflecting on some traditional playground games:

- What is the aim of each game?
- How many people can play?
- What do players have to do?
- Is there a special layout for the game or space in which you play?
- Is there a winner?
- How do you win?

Encourage children to think about why these games are best suited to being played outdoors.

Next, split the class into an equal number of small groups or pairs. Ask each group to create a new outdoor game for another group. They will need to write out the instructions for their game so that their classmates can play the game without having it explained to them. They may also want to add in a plan of the layout which could be annotated.

Set a time limit to create their game (perhaps ten to fifteen minutes). The focus here is on the clarity of the instructions rather than the complexity of the game. Remind pupils that some of the best games, like tag, are very simple. Some prompts on a printout may be helpful here:

- What is the aim of the game?
- How many can play?
- Is it a team game or for individuals?
- What do you have to do?
- Does equipment or markings have to be set out in a specific way? How might you make this clear for those trying out the game?
- Is there a specific order for things to take place?
- Is there a winner?
- How do you win?

Once the time is up, get the pairs to swap clipboards and read the instructions for their classmates' game. Once they have done this give them one minute to ask any clarifying questions. This will give pupils an opportunity to assess the clarity of the instructions they have written and understand where they might need to improve. After the minute for questions, each group should try out the game they have been given the instructions for. They can offer feedback to each other on the quality of the game instructions and their enjoyment of the new game so that these can be updated and improved before being handed over to another group to try out or being demonstrated to the wider class.

You may wish to choose the class's favourite new game and introduce this to break and lunchtime activities.

Progression and extensions:

This activity could have a specific numeracy or literacy focus by setting parameters for the game, such as having to include scoring or timing as part of the game. It could also be used to support health and wellbeing outcomes by exploring ways of giving feedback to others in a constructive and supportive manner.

Adaptations:

You could link this activity to a variety of learning contexts, investigating games from different periods in history or exploring traditional games from other parts of the world.

My outdoor diary

Subject area: Language and literacy

Key focus: Writing for different audiences.

Also
- sharing experiences, feelings, ideas and information in a way that communicates my message
- developing observational skills through using our different senses
- exploring different ways of recording my experiences

Level: Low

Previous learning required:

This activity will be revisited as pupils visit your outdoor spaces and should ideally be conducted regularly over a number of weeks.

Aim of the activity:

To use our experiences in nature to create a diary to share with our caregivers.

Equipment:

- a template page to prompt diary entries (see description below);
- clipboards, paper and pencils or whiteboards and markers.

Description of the activity:

Allow time as you visit your outdoor spaces each week to complete an outdoor diary. Create a template with the children to record the changes they see in their environment over time. They could include a space to draw a picture or add a photograph and boxes to record:

- pupil name;
- date and time;
- area of outdoor space visited;
- weather;
- what we were learning;
- any significant events;
- wildlife spotted;
- anything new in our environment;

This doesn't have to be a lengthy activity and it often works best if it forms part of your routine. It can be particularly effective to complete the diary entry at the end of a session outdoors to allow your pupils to reflect on their learning and encourage their observational skills for the next visit.

Towards the end of the term collate the diary entries and have pupils design a front cover. The completed diaries can be sent home to inform caregivers about the outdoor learning and play their children have been engaging in and provide an opportunity to revisit learning in the home environment.

Progression and extensions:

The observations your pupils have made can go on to form the basis of future learning or projects. For example, if the children have noticed an increase in litter over the term, they may want to take part in a litter-picking activity or awareness campaign in the wider school community.

Adaptations:

Completing a diary entry as part of your outdoor learning and play routine gives pupils the opportunity to record all sorts of information relevant to their learning. If you're learning about the water cycle you may want to record rainfall levels as part of your diary. If you're learning about minibeasts you may want to record sightings to find the best spots to return to later. Adapt the boxes on your template to suit the needs of your pupils and your school grounds.

Eco-activists

Subject area: Language and literacy

Key focus: Writing for different audiences

Also
- understanding how to present an argument using persuasive language and evidence
- developing a professional tone
- analysing and recording information

Level: High

Previous learning required:

This activity will build on existing language and literacy skills and will work most effectively in response to an issue pupils have already identified in their local environment through time spent in outdoor learning and play.

Aim of the activity:

To develop a persuasive argument in the form of a letter or email to organisations or individuals in the community about the need for action in the local environment.

Equipment:

- clipboards, paper and pencils or whiteboards and markers;
- access to a PC/laptop to type up and print or email letters.

Description of the activity:

Begin by discussing environmental concerns within the local community with your pupils. Are there areas where rubbish is dumped? Would they like more space for recycling? Perhaps they have identified an area of grass which could be left to grow longer to encourage biodiversity, or they want to encourage more people to use public transport?

Take your pupils outside. You may be able to observe your subject from the playground or go for a walk in the streets nearby before stopping to reflect. Divide your pupils into pairs and ask them to complete a SWOT (Strengths, Weaknesses, Opportunities and Threats) analysis of the area. It is helpful to decide in advance the scope of your projects; the idea here is to keep it local and achievable. Draw a cross in the centre of a page of A4 paper then label each quadrant.

- Strengths – What are we doing well?
- Weaknesses – What isn't working well?
- Opportunities – What could we do?
- Threats – What's stopping us?

Once you have identified some key areas where pupils have concerns or ideas for positive action, take a vote to decide which areas to focus on first.

Have pupils research their area of concern and come up with some solutions. Encourage them to think about who they need to speak to about a particular issue. Is it the local authority or council? Is it the public transport provider? Perhaps they need to write to the local paper or to a local business about a particular concern. Research the names and addresses of organisations online.

Next, have pupils write a letter detailing their concerns and how they think the issue might be addressed. Stress the importance of being polite and courteous and using evidence to back up any claims. Send them off, physically or digitally, and make a note to follow up on any responses.

Progression and extensions:

Depending on the success of their campaigns, pupils may want to branch out and tackle other issues in the community. Equally, they may have been ignored, but there is valuable learning in that as well. Use the opportunity to have a conversation about respectful dialogue and consider other ways to engage people in the things which concern us. It may lead to useful discussions about democracy, politics and responsible citizenship.

Adaptations:

The SWOT analysis is a useful approach to many issues and also for recording pupils' voices. It could be used to assess the opportunities to increase biodiversity within the school grounds or identify areas where gardening projects could take place.

A hunt for the truth

Subject area: Language and literacy

Key focus: Understanding the difference between truths, opinions and falsehoods

Level: Low

Previous learning required:

Understanding that a fact is the same as something that is true and can be trusted or proven.
   An opinion is not always true. Sometimes these have been created for entertainment, for example in a story, or are the way that a person *feels* about something.
   Something that is false can be proven to be wrong and should not be trusted as an argument or evidence.

Aim of the activity:

To determine whether sentences are made up of facts or fiction.

Equipment:

- a trail of written sentences and statements that can be placed around an outside area

Description of the activity:

To help the younger pupils to learn the difference between facts and opinions, take them on a hunt around your school grounds. You will need to tailor-make a trail around your site that is safe and suitable for your pupils to follow and includes relevant facts and information about your grounds. You can prepare this in advance and place the sentences along the trail, or simply share them with the group as you reach each place. Ensure that a range of different language is used, and include some clues to suggest whether a sentence might be true, an opinion or definitely false.

Example sentences:

- The tallest flowers in the field are the most pretty.
- The climbing frame is painted red.
- Mrs Johnson thinks the benches are the best place to sit.
- There are five trees in the wooded area.
- The surface of the playground is soft and squishy.
- The year 6 classroom is the closest to the water fountain.

With each sentence, ask your pupils to look carefully at the area to find out if it is the truth or not. Ask if there are any clues in the words used in the sentence that could tell us whether it is fact or opinion. Discuss why it is important to understand the difference between truths and non-truths and why each might be used at different times in what we say or write.

Progression and extensions:

Add in some sentences from stories that your pupils will know or some facts about particular species found in your school grounds. As an extension, ask your pupils to make up their own sentences (facts or opinion) and test them on each other.

Adaptations:

For less able pupils who you want to complete the activity independently, you could use photos instead of sentences. Some pictures could be of your school grounds and some of other outdoor areas. Your pupils must try to find the pictures that are 'true' and actually in their grounds, while discarding the 'false' ones.

Reflecting on outdoor experiences

Subject area: Language and literacy

Key focus: Writing from personal experience

Also
- reflecting on how different places and activities make you feel
- writing in a consistent tense

Level: High

Previous learning required:

How to write in the first person. Pupils must have completed some outdoor learning so that they can reflect on these experiences.

Aim of the activity:

To write about personal outdoor experiences.

Equipment:

- clipboards, paper and pencils or whiteboards and markers.

Description of the activity:

This activity should be done outside so that your pupils can remember how they feel when they are in the natural setting of their school grounds.

Make sure everyone has a way to mark down ideas and ask your pupils to sit individually in an area that you have used a lot for outdoor learning, so they have space for personal reflections. To help them plan what they are going to write about, question your pupils and discuss some activities that they have completed over the years of their school life. Alongside each of these activities, encourage them to note adjectives to describe how they felt while they were outside doing these lessons. Prompt them as to whether their feelings and emotions have changed as they have gained more experience in using the grounds for learning and, if so, what they think may have caused these changes. Remind your pupils to think about their own personal feelings and experiences rather than as a group and to be as honest as possible in their reflections.

It can also be useful to think about all their different senses and how these were affected by being in a different learning environment. Ask them to think about reasons why they may have felt in a particular way or experienced a certain emotion. Encourage ideas about how being outside rather than inside makes them feel generally – does it help them with their learning, encourage them to work together or even help them to concentrate when back in the classroom?

Once they have brainstormed ideas and planned their writing, allow your pupils time to write up their personal reflections on their outdoor experiences.

Progression and extensions:

Challenge your pupils to think about what outdoor experiences they would like to have in the future and add these to the final paragraph of their writing. They could also be extended to include a reflection about whether the outdoor learning they have experienced at school has changed the way they behave or interact with nature and the outdoors at home or with their family.

Adaptations:

This piece of writing can be used as a stimulus to demonstrate or practise any area of writing that you are focusing on. Target particular vocabulary, writing styles or grammar that you need to assess.

It can also either be written fully in the past tense or present tense, or used to show how to switch between the two.

Reading from a range of texts outdoors

Subject area: Language and literacy

THREE PROGRESSIVE ACTIVITIES

Key focus: Reading from a range of texts – a progression of suggested focus texts that can link to outdoor learning.

Also
- reading in different settings
- using texts as a stimulus for writing and other literacy activities

Level: Low, medium and high

Previous learning required:

This activity shows a range of different texts and genres of writing that can be used across the years. The suggested books can be explored as part of a cross-curricular topic that can prompt a range of activities and learning appropriate to the year group you are working with.

The source of writing can be chosen to best suit the needs of your pupils and, although part of this collection, they can, of course, be selected and used independently of each other. You may choose to use an extract from the text or to study the whole book.

This activity is designed to suggest useful texts and links that you can refer to when teaching reading. The suggested texts can also be used to inspire pupils and help develop an interest in both reading for pleasure and the natural world.

Aim of the activity:

To read from, understand and to recognise a range of texts.

Equipment:

The key to connecting pupils to what they are reading or listening to is to make sure they are comfortable. If they are reading independently or enjoying paired reading, let them choose where they want to sit so that they are relaxed and engaged. Try not to worry about their positioning and posture – think about where and how you like to read for pleasure! If possible, have some sit mats, log seats or tarpaulins available for them to sit on – especially if the weather has been wet.

If you are reading a text to your pupils in a group, position yourself so that they can all hear you clearly and see the book if you are sharing pictures. Be mindful of the weather and wind direction and gather the group in close if you need to. There is no point reading a story outside if they can't hear it!

The most suitable area to read in will depend on your grounds and may change depending on what you are reading. You may find sheltered spots, natural book nooks, wooded corners or even use purpose-built dens. Again, don't be afraid to let the children choose where they want to gather for their reading as they may have discovered suitable areas during their other lessons or break times. If possible, choose an area that matches the setting and genre of the text you are studying, for example a meadow for a poem about wildflowers, near to trees for stories set in a woodland, next to your raised beds for stories about growing vegetables or by your bug hotel and wildlife habitats for non-fiction texts about animals.

It can help to use books that are well worn when reading outside so that it doesn't matter if they get slightly damaged. Ask for donations of old books from the school community or pick up cheap second-hand books in charity shops or jumble sales.

Books and texts could be stored in boxes, baskets or waterproof bags so they can easily be transported to an outdoor setting. Encourage the transition of books from the classroom to outside so that pupils start to recognise that reading doesn't only take place indoors.

Description of the activities:

Listed below are groups of suggested texts for all levels of activities. These are not exhaustive and you may already be studying books that will lend themselves to being read outside. For each text there will be specific questions that will relate to the information or detail in the book. Below are some example questions that could be used for any text:

- Is the writing fiction or non-fiction?
- What is the purpose of the text?
- How does the writing make you feel?
- Does it help to listen/read the text or story in an outdoor setting? How is it different to being inside?
- Are there any similarities between the setting of the story or text and your school grounds?
- Have you ever been in the same situation or felt the same as the characters in the book?
- What language techniques or vocabulary has the writer used in the text and why?
- How would the story/text change if it wasn't set or linked to the outside?

There are a huge number of stories that link to outdoor settings and suggestions are listed below.

For non-fiction texts, it's helpful to utilise books about the natural world or things that your pupils may find in their school grounds. Use outdoor lesson sheets as a comprehension activity where the children can read the instructions and teach them to another group. Make use of identification charts and fact guides so your pupils can learn about nature while also reading a non-fiction text.

Lower-level activity:

Fiction

- Julia Donaldson – *Stick Man, Superworm, The Gruffalo*
- Rachel Bright – *The Squirrels Who Squabbled, Side by Side, The Lion Inside*
- Emily Gravett – *Tidy, Cave Baby*
- Paula Metcalf – *Rabbits Don't Lay Eggs*
- Lydia Monks – *Aaaaarrgghh! Spider!*
- Eric Carle – *The Very Hungry Caterpillar*
- Melanie Watt – *Scaredy Squirrel*
- Michael Rosen – *We're Going on a Bear Hunt*
- Fairytales and traditional stories – *Jack and the Beanstalk, Goldilocks* or *The Three Little Pigs*

Poetry/rhyming books

- Giles Andreae – *Mad about Minibeasts*
- Tony Mitton – *Twist and Hop, Minibeast Bop*
- Christina Rossetti – *What Is Pink?*

- Mary O'Neill – *What Is Green?*
- Shirley Hughes – *Out and About: A First Book of Poems*

Non-fiction

- Moira Butterfield and Jesus Verona – *Look What I Found in the Woods*
- Sebastian Braun – *Look and Say What You See in the Town*
- Simple identification charts with names and pictures of species to find and identify.

Middle-level activity:

Fiction

- Roald Dahl – *James and the Giant Peach, Danny the Champion of the World, George's Marvellous Medicine, Fantastic Mr Fox*
- Clive King – *Stig of the Dump* (potential link to history topics)
- Michael Morpurgo – *Where My Wellies Take Me*
- Dr Seuss – *The Lorax* (climate change and impacts)
- Julia Green – *The Wilderness War*

Poetry

- Robert Macfarlane – *The Lost Words, The Lost Spells*
- The National Trust – *I Am the Seed That Grew the Tree* (poetry collection)
- Alfred Lord Tennyson – *The Eagle*
- David Covell – *Run Wild*

Non-fiction

- Zoe Ingram – *My First Book of Birds*
- Celia Godkin – *Wolf Island* (based on true events)
- Fiona Danks – *The Stick Book*
- Learning through Landscapes – Activity sheets

Higher-level activity:

Fiction

- J. K. Rowling – the Harry Potter series
- E. B. White – *Charlotte's Web*
- C. S. Lewis – The Chronicles of Narnia
- Enid Blyton – The Magic Faraway Tree collection

- Gill Lewis – *Skyhawk*
- Michelle Paver – *Wolf Brother* (potential link to history topics)

Poetry

- Holly McNish – *Hidden Woods*
- Georgia Heard – *Awakening the Heart*
- Don Paterson – *Rain, Two Trees*

Non-fiction

- *Collins Complete Guide to British Wildlife*
- Lily Dyer – *Earth Heroes*
- Classification identification charts – available online

Progression and extensions:

Once pupils have read outside, there is a multitude of follow-up activities that you could complete. Listening to or reading outside could provide a stimulus for them to write their own stories, poems or non-chronological reports. They could create characters or scenes from natural materials outside or act out parts of the story in a wide-open space. They could make an alternative setting for the book or make pictures that would support the text if they don't already exist. Challenge your pupils to write what they thought happened before or after the main part of the story or change the genre of the text by writing a fact book about the fiction characters. Or ask them to write a story about the animals and creatures found in the identification charts/fact sheets.

Adaptations:

For those who may find it difficult to follow oral texts, sections of pages of the books can help them to be able to refer back to pages or look at the pictures more closely. These could be pegged on a washing line so that your pupils can follow the order as they listen. This can also help if you have limited copies of texts available.

Ask your pupils to think about other books or stories they may have read or heard of that take place in an outdoor setting. They may have used spotter guides or books outside of school or seen family members using them. Explain that even as adults we will often find things outside that we need to look up and that is how we learn new things. Encourage your pupils to bring in any examples of outdoor texts or stories that they have used in the past.

Some pupils will benefit from reading being available as an activity during breaktimes and lunchtime, not simply during reading lessons. A designated reading area, outdoor library or fact sheets/identification charts would encourage this and help to develop a love of reading.

LANGUAGE AND LITERACY ACTIVITIES CAN ALSO BE FOUND WITHIN THE FOLLOWING THEMES:

- Grow, cook, eat, celebrate – retrieving information from different sources, writing from personal experience, campfire stories;
- Dig for Victory – writing diaries of the garden, making radio jingles, training another group, writing scientific or practical advice on growing;
- Pollination – descriptive language, researching using different sources and identifying facts, writing for different audiences and for different reasons;
- The Vikings have arrived – storytelling and writing;
- Seasonal change – diaries and journals, Looking from here …, the sporting year.

10
Maths and numeracy

INTRODUCING MATHS AND NUMERACY OUTDOORS

Going outside can really help you make maths come alive for your class. There is so much maths outdoors just sitting there to be discovered and measured, from the temperature outside each day to the height of the trees in your grounds, from the angles in playground markings to the symmetry in flowers. Then there is the data you can collect from undertaking different activities: How long does it take to run from one end of the playground to the other? What is the average length of twig found in the grounds? How much does our harvest of potatoes weigh this year?

All this amazing data can then be presented in different forms including graphs, tables and charts, and it can be analysed in numerous ways. Creating real data that has real meaning for your pupils to manipulate rather than lists of numbers in a book can help to reinforce principles and practices in ways that maintain the interest of your pupils because they have collected the information themselves.

But this is just the start. Why not use free natural resources to represent number values or mathematical symbols? How about working on a large scale to create your charts, tables and graphs on the playground or field? Mathematical vocabulary can also be developed outdoors: *count* the number of trees, *estimate* the length of the field, what is the *product* of the length of runner beans and their number, explore the *patterns* in the brickwork, this leaf is *the same length as* my hand and so on.

Having real lengths and weights to measure and real problems to solve can also be possible indoors but you will always be limited with space and the resources you can use inside. Outdoors you can measure long lengths using metres instead of centimetres, use water to check volumes and not worry about splashing it on the floor and even embody shapes and angles with plenty of space to make things as large as you can.

Outdoor number lines

Subject area: Maths and numeracy

Key focus: Number – understanding and using negative numbers

Also
- using number lines as a written method for addition and subtraction

Level: Medium

Previous learning required:

Using number lines as a method for addition and subtraction.
An understanding of negative numbers and where they would fit on a number line.

Aim of the activity:

To practically use human-scale number lines to show the transition from positive to negative numbers.

Equipment:

- a concrete space/playground;
- a number line if you have one (you can mark one out in chalk if you don't);
- chalk;
- masking tape/rope, metre rulers (optional).

Description of the activity:

Remind pupils that negative numbers are less than 0 and of their numerical pattern as they decrease. To demonstrate this, show a thermometer with negative temperatures on so that pupils can see what happens when the temperature increases or decreases.

You may have existing straight lines marked on your playground that can be utilised, such as sports courts or pitch markings. You may also have a number line in your grounds that can be extended. Alternatively, ask small groups to draw straight lines first, using metre rulers to help them. Ask the children to mark 0 on the centre of their line and next, where you would land if you added 1 or took 1 away. Challenge your pupils to continue their creation and draw a number line that goes from −10 to +10.

Use these number lines to demonstrate what happens when you add to or take away from both positive and negative numbers. Set a variety of questions that make your pupils cross 0 and allow them to physically move up or down the number line, standing on the starting number and moving through the markings to see where they land.

Progression and extensions:

When your pupils are confident using the initial number lines they have created, challenge them to make one that has a further range, for example −50 to +50. This can then be used for more challenging calculations.

As a further progression, your pupils could use a blank number line where they mark their calculations (jumps) according to where they land. Ensure they are given questions that force them to cross the 0 and move between negative and positive numbers.

Using these large number lines is a natural step and easy transition into using written number lines to show calculations in workbooks.

Adaptations:

If you do not have any chalk or access to an asphalt space, you could use masking tape or rope to create your number line instead. Your pupils could mark the numbers by using natural materials to form the number labels.

If your pupils are struggling with which way to move up and down the number line, ask them to use the chalk or natural items to make reminder signs or arrows on the playground to show which way to move for addition or subtraction. If needed, practise simpler calculations first that do not cross the 0 or involve negative numbers so that your pupils get used to the method. Your outdoor number lines can be used to support any number work and adapted to whatever focus you are working on.

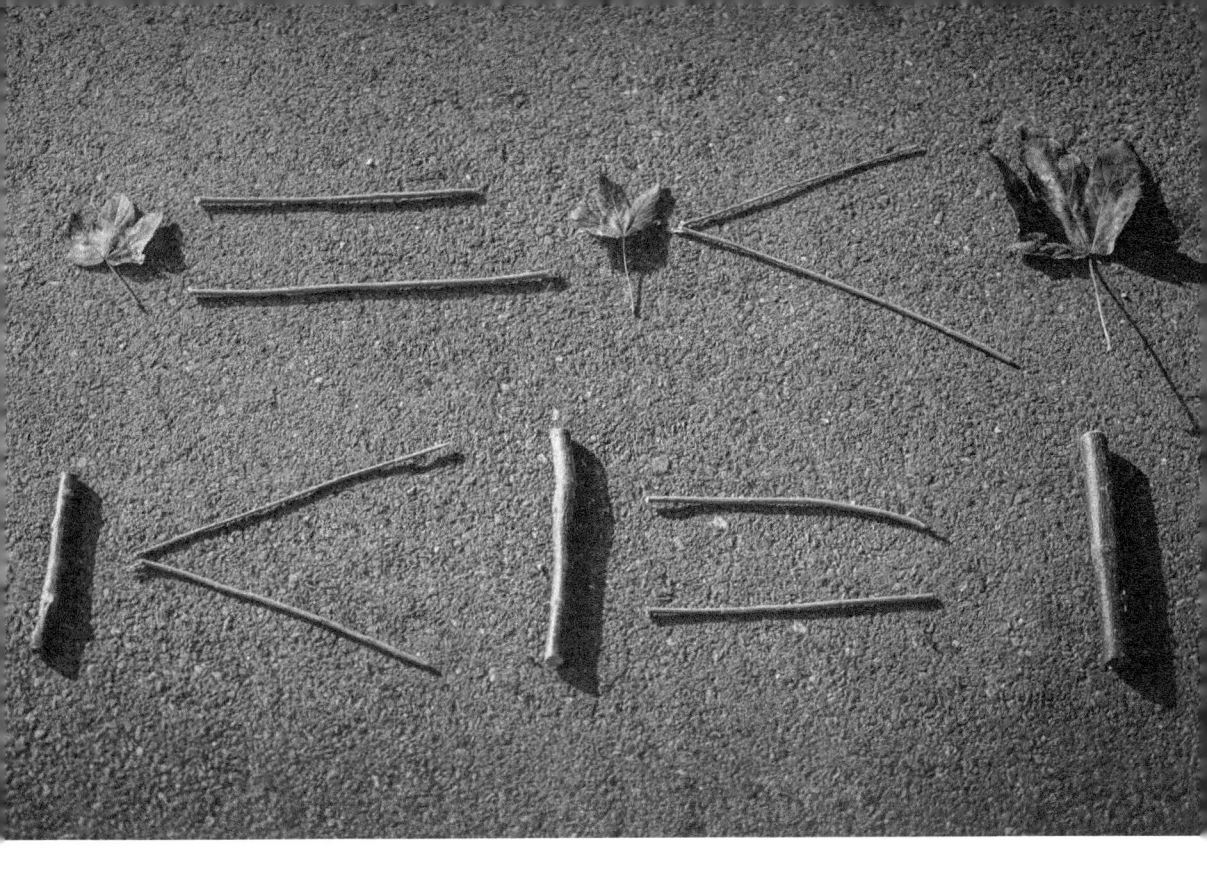

Size comparisons

Subject area: Maths and numeracy

Key focus: Estimating, calculating and measuring – length

Also
- using the terms and signs for greater than and less than
- using mathematical language to compare sizes
- looking for similarities and differences between items and creating repeated patterns

Level: Low

Previous learning required:

Understanding the vocabulary of measurement, such as bigger, smaller, length and width.

Aim of the activity:

To use mathematical terms to compare sizes and sort natural items.

Equipment:

- a selection of natural items such as leaves and sticks;
- chalk (optional).

Description of the activity:

Give your pupils a couple of minutes at the start of the lesson to collect some natural materials such as sticks and leaves and place them in the middle of the area you are using. Ask them to choose one item to start with and to place it in front of them. Then, ask them all to pick another item that is bigger than the original one they have and to also place it on the ground in front of them. Next, ask them to choose something smaller than their original item and place that on the ground too. Talk about the patterns they can see forming in their chosen items and see if they can add to them.

Challenges can be set, such as finding the biggest or smallest items, sorting just the leaves or just the sticks, or giving them a set number to find and put in size order.

Discuss whether we always all agree on which is biggest or smallest and if there are any that are hard to put in order of size and why. Think about and discuss the difference between the width and length of an item and ask the children to explore whether this makes a difference to the order you would put things in. Finally, encourage your pupils to think about how they could make sure they are getting it right rather than just using their eyes.

Progression and extensions:

Use greater than, less than and equals signs to extend your pupils' learning. You could draw the signs on the playground with chalk or create them out of sticks. Pupils can then lay their natural items on the correct side of the sign to make accurate number sentences. For example, this stick is a greater length than this stick or there are an equal number of leaves on each side. This is a great concrete way of exploring these signs and a basis for using them with abstract numbers.

Adaptations:

This activity could also be used to look for patterns and to group items together. Encourage your pupils to look for similarities and differences between the items they have found and decide on a variety of ways to group them together, for example shape, colour, size.

Pupils could also use natural items to demonstrate their knowledge of patterns by placing them into a repeating order, for example stick, stick, leaf, stick, stick, leaf. If possible, photograph the children's work to evidence the learning in their books.

Den dimensions

Subject area: Maths and numeracy

Key focus: Estimating, calculating and measuring – area

Also
- geometry, properties of shapes
- measurement of different shapes

Level: Medium

Previous learning required:

Measuring length. Calculating the area of regular shapes.

Aim of the activity:

To use knowledge of area to design and build a den for a small group of pupils.

Equipment:

- long tape measures;
- rope or string, or chalk if planning work is done on a hard surface;
- den building equipment such as poles and long sticks, bungie ropes and ties, string or rope, old sheets and blankets, clothes pegs;
- clipboards and pencils or whiteboards and markers.

Description of the activity:

In this activity pupils will work in small teams to design a den that will accommodate a given number of pupils (2–4 is enough). They will first have to work out how much space they will need, then design and build their den.

The first task is to find out how much space will be needed per person. To do this they should ask one of their group to sit down on the ground and then mark out a square around them. Ask them to measure carefully so that it is a square – this may mean that they have more space around their body in one direction. They will have to decide whether they want a lot of space around each person or whether it will be a tight fit in their den. The bigger the area, the bigger the den they will need to build. Have they considered how high the den will need to be? And what happens if the walls slope inwards?

Pupils should then calculate the area of the square they have made – this is the area per person they need for their den. They should then multiply this by the number of people they want in their den.

Discuss how they can then plan their den to fit the right number of people. They will need to work out how big the floor space needs to be, measure and mark it out, and build their den accordingly.

Once their den is completed, they can see if they can fit the expected number of people inside it.

Take a tour of all the dens and review which were most successful and discuss why that is. Let pupils return to their own dens to make improvements.

If you can, leave the dens outside for break or lunchtime so that pupils can play in them.

Progression and extensions:

With more able pupils, consider measuring and using areas that are not squares – including rectangles. How does this affect the design of the den?

Adaptations:

Instead of making dens you can make a simple seating area. Use paper to mark out your space or cardboard if you would like it to be a bit more robust.

Various volumes

Subject area: Maths and numeracy

Key focus: Estimating, calculating and measuring – volume

Also
- working scientifically

Level: High

Previous learning required:

Measuring length and calculating volume.
Multiplication of numbers with decimal places.

Aim of the activity:

To estimate, calculate and measure the volume of different containers.

Equipment:

- a selection of waterproof containers with straight, vertical sides – small containers for the groups, a larger container for the demonstration;
- for the main activity use rectangular containers, for the progression use cylinders;
- tape measures or rulers;
- water;
- measuring jugs;
- clipboards, paper and pencils;
- a worksheet with a table showing:
    - Container shape;
    - Estimated volume;
    - Measurements from the container – length, width and depth;
    - Calculated volume;
    - Volume of water contained.
- Calculators.

Description of the activity:

This is a great activity to do outside as it allows for spillages of water along the way. The aim is to estimate then measure the volume of different containers, then to check out how accurate this was by filling them up with water to measure.

When you know you want to do this activity, start collecting containers – small or large. They need to have straight sides (not sloping) and be waterproof so that the water doesn't leak out of them.

Start with a demonstration. Use a large container so that everyone can see what is going on. Ask for an estimation of the volume of the container, then measure the length, width and depth of the container on the inside – ask your pupils why this matters. Calculate the volume and say that you are going to check this by filling it up with water. You can then either measure out water into the container using a measuring jug or fill it up and empty it with the jug. Get your pupils involved at every stage in the demonstration.

How close to your calculation did you get? Why might the calculation and the measurement be slightly different?

Next, hand out a selection of rectangular containers, measuring jugs, rulers or tapes, calculators and clipboards, paper and pencils to small groups. Make sure they also have access to water.

Each group should estimate then take measurements and calculate the volume of their containers before filling them with water and pouring this out into the measuring jugs to see how much they hold. All these findings should be recorded on their worksheets.

As a class, they findings should put their shapes in order of volume along a line and discuss how similar or different the volume of different containers was – that a tall, thin container may hold a similar amount to a short fat one, for example.

Progression and extensions:

Use cylinders and calculate the volume using area of the base x height ($\pi r^2 h$).

Compare different shapes and ask pupils to guess which will hold the most water before they measure them or test them out by transferring water between containers.

Adaptations:

Keep your eye out for different containers with sides that can be measured in whole numbers as this will make the maths easier. You can also set out the equation on worksheets so that pupils fill in the numbers measured and undertake the calculations more easily.

The human bar chart

Subject area: Maths and numeracy

Key focus: Charts, tables and graphs

Level: Low

Previous learning required:

Number and place values

Aim of the activity:

To introduce the idea of a bar chart in practical form before transferring information to paper.

Equipment:

- if working on the playground – chalk;
- if working on the grass – rope, string or lengths of cloth.

Description of the activity:

In this activity, pupils will be using their own data or data collected from around the grounds to create bar charts using their own bodies. They will then transfer this information to paper.

On the ground, lay out vertical and horizontal positive axes and mark out equal divisions along the bottom line. To be more accurate, create a grid on the ground for pupils to stand in; this will also make it easier to transfer the information to paper. Make the grid lighter in colour so that the axes stand out.

The next job is to collect some data. This can be as simple as what your pupils had for breakfast, the month in which they were born or their favourite colour. Or why not run an activity in which simple data is collected, such as the distance a ball is thrown by each member of the class? The important thing is that each person has one piece of data that is theirs alone.

Each column on your bar chart is then an answer. This could be a range of data, for example birthdays in January to March, April to June, July to September, October to December or up to 5m, 5–10m, 10–15m, 15–20m and over 20m for the distance a ball is thrown. Or each column can represent one piece of data, for example red, green, blue, black or grey cars.

Each pupil stands in a line in the column that represents their piece of data – spaced out by standing in the grid. Straight away they will see that the column is longer the more people who share the data. So if 10 people were born between January and March and only five between October and December the former column would have twice as many people in as the latter and therefore be twice as long.

If you can view the chart from above you could take photographs so that the information can be seen even more clearly.

Run this activity several times with different data and record the results.

When back inside, transfer the information onto paper and compare what this looks like with what it looked like made up of people.

Progression and extensions:

Pupils can set up their own bar charts working in groups and collecting their own data. They can also analyse the data in different ways or rearrange the parameters to see how that changes the results, for example birthdays between February and April, May and August and so on.

Adaptations:

Instead of using people you can use objects found in your grounds, for example pebbles or pine cones, and work on a smaller scale.

Exploring angles

Subject area: Maths and numeracy

Key focus: Geometry – exploring and demonstrating angles

Also
- showing the correct positions of right angles, acute, obtuse and reflex angles and straight lines
- understanding and applying knowledge of the properties of each type of angle

Level: Medium

Previous learning required:

Understanding that:

- a right angle is 90°;
- an acute angle is less than 90°;

- an obtuse angle is between 90° and 180°;
- a straight line has an angle of 180°;
- a reflex angle is between 180° and 360°;
- a full or complete angle is 360°;

Aim of the activity:

To demonstrate knowledge and understanding of the properties of angles.

Equipment:

- a large open space;
- sticks (optional);
- chalk (optional).

Description of the activity:

Start by reminding your pupils of the different angle names that you have been working on and also how many degrees are in each angle. Demonstrate each one practically by using your arms and get your pupils to copy and show each angle too. Next, challenge them to see if they can make a right angle with the rest of their body, for example by using their legs or by hinging at the waist. Ask them all to demonstrate their attempts and talk about the different methods shown. Explain that for some angles it may be easier to make them by working together in pairs or even small groups. Divide the group into small teams and set them challenges to create various types of angles. They could receive points for each one correctly demonstrated, or for correctly guessing the angles that other teams have made. Encourage them to experiment with different techniques and reassure them that it is OK to get active or to lie on the ground.

Progression and extensions:

To extend the learning, try out some angle aerobics where your pupils have to turn and change position by allocated angles. Start by just asking them to turn 90° and then move onto 180° or 360°, acute, obtuse or reflex. You could even set up an obstacle course or maze and ask your pupils to challenge each other to get to a designated point by completing various turns. Make sure these properties are always related back to the correct terms for each angle.

Adaptations:

This activity could also be done using sticks or chalk instead of body parts. The sticks could be laid out into different angles on the playground for your pupils to label using chalk. They could also hunt for various angles around the school grounds and find examples of each, for example in trees, on fences or in playground markings. These could be sketched or photographed to be labelled and identified.

Measuring outdoor circles

Subject area: Maths and numeracy

Key focus: Creating circles and measuring their features.

Also
- recognising and locating circles in the real world

Level: High

Previous learning required:

Knowing that a circle is a 2D curved shape, where every point is the same distance from the centre.
Understanding how to recognise the radius, diameter and circumference of a circle.

Aim of the activity:

To use measuring equipment to explore and measure some of the features of circles.

Equipment:

- a concrete or asphalt space;
- string/rope;
- chalk;
- measuring equipment such as rules/tape measures;
- clipboards, paper and pencils or whiteboards and markers.

Description of the activity:

Explain to your pupils that you are going to explore the properties of some circles while working outside, but you first need to draw the circles. Split the class into small groups and ensure that each group has some chalk and rope or string. Ask them to attach the string around the chalk at one end so that it will still draw. To demonstrate how to use the technique, ask all the children to measure 1 metre of their string and for one member of the group to hold the point that is exactly 1 metre away from the chalk. This person will become the centre of the circle, while another pupil pulls the string taut and draws the circle with the chalk. The person in the middle will need to turn around as their partner moves the chalk around the circle. Talk to your pupils about how we know this has drawn a circle 1 metre distance to the centre all the way around. Ask them what the radius of this circle is (1m) and also if anyone can calculate the diameter (2m).

Once your pupils know the technique, give them tasks to draw circles with a different radius. Challenge them by giving a diameter rather than a radius and see if they can work out how to draw the circle (halve the diameter measurement to find the radius and therefore length of string needed).

Each group could draw various size circles before swapping over. The other groups could then measure and label the features of their drawings to check they have completed their tasks correctly.

Progression and extensions:

Challenge your pupils to find out the circumference of the circles they have drawn and remind them that this is the distance around the outside edge. This can be done by placing string or rope around the circumference of the circle as this can be flexed into place. This string can then be straightened out and placed alongside a ruler or measuring tape to calculate the length of the circumference.

Adaptations:

If you are limited by space or don't have any chalk available, your pupils could find circles that exist in their outdoor setting and measure the features of these. Remind them to look out for cylinders, which will have circular faces that could be measured.

Items that you will have around the school could be useful, such as hoops, tyres, manhole covers, cones or skipping ropes that are or can create circles. Again, pupils could go on a hunt for these or bring them back to be measured.

Discovering pi

Subject area: Maths and numeracy

Key focus: Geometry

Also
- rearranging equations
- the geometry of circles
- understanding degrees of error

Level: High

Previous learning required:

- Knowledge of how to calculate the area of straight-sided shapes.
- Drawing circles (see 'Measuring outdoor circles').

Aim of the activity:

To help pupils understand the concept of pi and how they can use it to calculate the circumference or area of a circle.

Equipment:

- chalk and string to mark out circles on hard surfaces or string or rope to mark out circles on grass;
- long tape measures and/or measuring wheels;
- calculators;
- clipboard and pencils – with a table with three columns headed: circumference, diameter and one left blank at the end (this will be for pi).

Description of the activity:

This leads on well from the previous activity of drawing circles and measuring their radius and circumference.

'Discovering' pi is something you can do with your pupils combining practical activity with mathematical processes to help them understand how to use this constant when working with circles and cylinders.

Remember that pi is a ratio between the circumference of a circle and the diameter of that circle. It is the same for every circle, which means that when we know either the diameter of a circle or its circumference we can calculate the other dimension. All you need to know to do this is the formula $C = \prod d$ – (or $C = 2\prod r$) with C being the circumference and d being the diameter, $\prod$ (pi) is a constant (r being the radius). So if we rearrange this equation we can find that if you divide the circumference of a circle by its diameter you will find $\prod$ (pi). $C/d = \prod$ (or $C/2r$). So start by showing your class the first formula and then ask them how they can find $\prod$ if they know the circumference and diameter of a circle. Write this equation in the third column on the recording sheet.

Once they have worked this out, go outside and, in small groups, pupils should draw large circles on the ground. The bigger the circles, the less any errors will affect your results as they will be proportionately smaller the larger the circle. This is why it is impossible to do this activity inside as you can't draw large enough circles for errors to not impact your results.

Your pupils then need to measure the circumference and the diameter of their circle. Remember the diameter has to go through the middle of the circle – or they can measure the radius and multiply this by 2. They should add their results to the recording sheet and calculate what they think pi is.

The next task is to find the average of everyone's calculations for pi – the more circles you use, the more the error will be evened out. Your answer should be approximately 3.14. Discuss why you might not have got this exact answer (errors drawing or in measuring) and that pi is always 3.14, so that whatever circle you have, you can work out its circumference if you know its diameter.

Progression and extensions:

Moving on from finding the area of a circle, you can find the volume of a cylinder by multiplying the area of its end with its height.

Why not celebrate pi day on March 14th (3.14 – third month, fourteenth day) and undertake lots of activities focusing on circles?

Adaptations:

Are there natural or man-made circles in your grounds? Why not see if you can use these too? Because they are likely to be smaller your errors are likely to be larger, but if you are limited with space this is a good starting point.

Folding fractions

Subject area: Maths and numeracy

Key focus: Fractions – recognising and finding fractions of a half and a quarter

Also
- understanding that fractions are sharing equal parts of a whole object or number

Level: Low

Previous learning required:

Learning that a half is when we split something into two equal parts and a third is three equal parts and so on.

Aim of the activity:

To practically demonstrate how to find fractions in shapes.

Equipment:

- a large open space;
- a variety of sheets, tarpaulins or blankets;
- chalk or masking tape (optional).

Description of the activity:

Lay out a tarpaulin on the ground and ask your pupils if they can think of a way that they could find half of it. Explain that as we know a half is when we split a shape into two equal parts, we can fold the tarp in half together to find what half the shape looks like (just like if we cut a sandwich, pizza or cake in half!). If you have sheets or tarps of the same size, this half could be laid back down on to the original (whole) shape, so that you can visually see what the difference is. Different colour sheets will work well to contrast the different areas. You could also experiment with moving the half around on the original shape and see if it can be in a different position. Explore if there are any other ways that the tarpaulin could be folded into two equal parts. Challenge your pupils to fold their sheet into quarters, always reminding them to make sure they are equal parts. If you have different shape materials such as circular, this can be a nice example too. Give your pupils time to experiment with different ways of folding the sheets and let them decide whether they think they have created chosen or given fractions or not, depending on whether they have folded it equally.

Progression and extensions:

This activity could be extended to finding fractions of amounts. Once your pupils know how to find half of the tarps/sheet shape, you could challenge them to mark this using chalk or tape. You could then start exploring fractions of amounts using natural materials as counters. For example, to find a quarter of 12, ask your pupils to collect 12 leaves. Fold the tarpaulin into quarters and mark these equal areas. Now share the 12 leaves equally between the four sections and see how many are in each quarter.

Adaptations:

If you do not have access to a range of tarpaulins or blankets, you could use existing playground markings or draw shapes on the concrete. Your pupils could then be challenged to find and use chalk to colour in the fraction that you give them. Alternatively, they could have to stand or lie in an area covering the fraction you ask for.

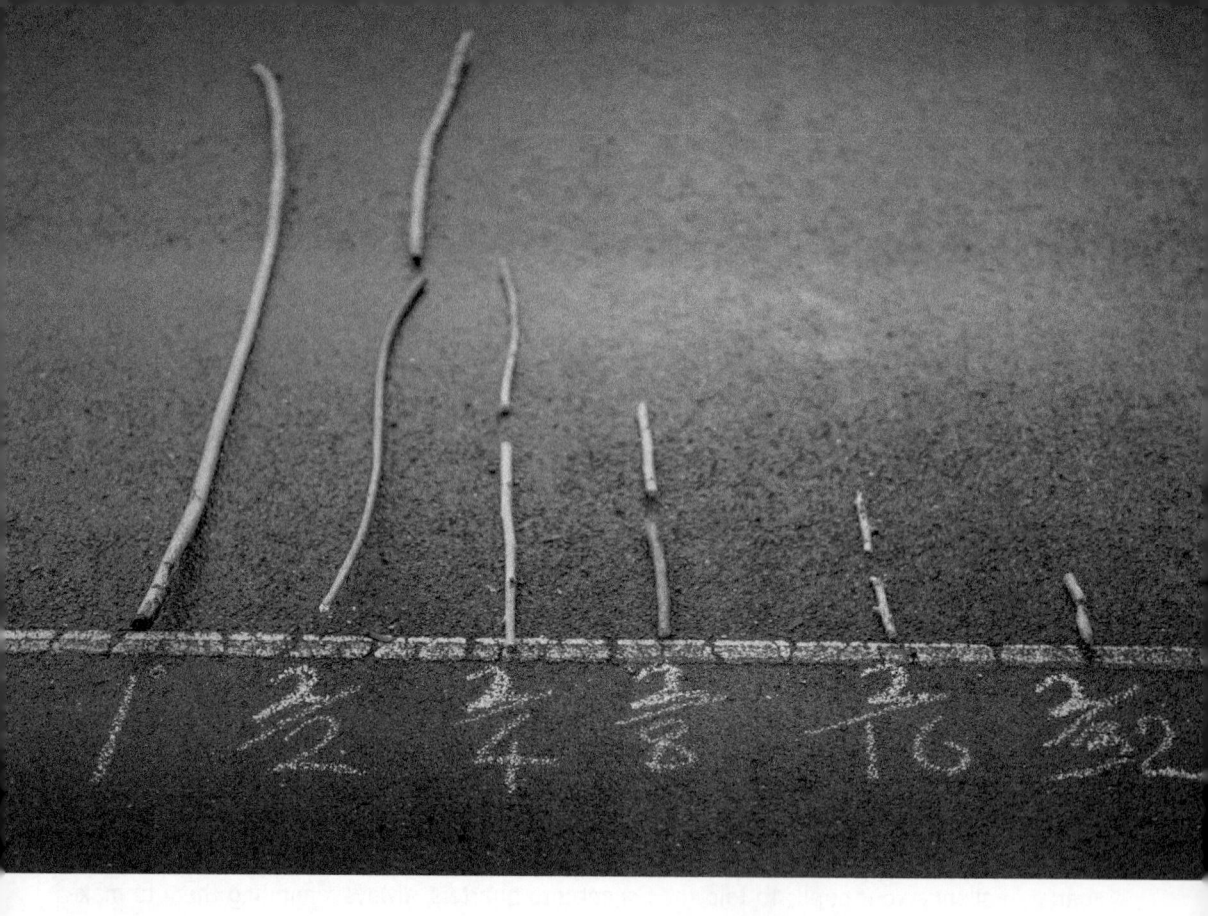

Stick fraction walls

Subject area: Maths and numeracy

Key focus: Fractions – recognising and demonstrating fractions

Also
- understanding that fractions are sharing equal parts of a whole object or number
- measuring and comparing sizes

Level: Medium

Previous learning required:

Knowing that a half is when we split something into two equal parts, a third is three equal parts etc.

It would be useful if your pupils have seen and experienced a fraction wall before the activity, so they are familiar with the concept.

Aim of the activity:

To practically create a fraction wall from natural materials.

Equipment:

- a variety of sticks of different sizes;
- white paper or sheets to place sticks and fraction walls on so they are more visible and pencils to write the values of the fractions (optional);
- secateurs (optional).

Description of the activity:

Ask your pupils to collect one of the largest sticks they can find. Explain that this is going to be their whole or 1 at the top of their fraction wall. Next, ask your pupils to think about what they would need to consider in making the next layer of their fraction wall – halves. Emphasise the need for the two sticks to be the same size as each other and to make up the total length of the whole. Highlight that as you are working with natural materials, it may not be possible to be 100% accurate, but they must try to make their fraction walls as accurate as possible. Once they have found two sticks for the halves, let them find three for thirds, four for quarters, etc. to complete their wall. You can also ask pupils to label each of the fractions.

If you are working with pupils who have done some tool work before and you feel they are safe to do so, have secateurs available so they can trim sticks down to the correct length. Alternatively, adults could have secateurs to help cut sticks if pupils really struggle to find one that is the correct length.

Progression and extensions:

Once the groups have made their fraction walls, ask them to remove a few of their 'parts' (fraction sticks) and place them to the side of their completed walls. As groups swap over, they have to work out what the missing fraction is from the length they have left behind – do they need a half of their '1' a third of a quarter for example. They can then either replace it from the side or write the missing fraction part in the space that's left. Remind them that they should be able to calculate this by counting how many other parts are on that row of the fraction wall or check with the labels they have made for each stick fraction.

Adaptations:

Once completed, you could ask your pupils to label the sticks with marker pens or coloured labels so that they can be used as a learning resource for later lessons.

If you do not have access to natural materials these could be brought onto site from elsewhere and used as a resource for outdoor lessons. Alternatively, cut up some strips of fabric or old sheets/tarps that could be used for this activity. The same learning could also be achieved by allowing the children to use chalk on the playground and draw their fraction walls.

Exploring number and place value through natural materials

Subject area: Maths and numeracy

PROGRESSIVE ACTIVITIES

Key focus: Number and place value

Also
- count, read, write and know the value of whole numbers
- recognising that the place of a digit indicates its value

- solve problems using concrete objects and representations
- understand that a letter or symbol can stand for an unknown number
- express missing number problems using different resources

Level: Low, medium and high

Previous learning required:

This activity shows progression across the years – so pupils start with basic number activities and move on to more complex methods and ideas as they move up the school. Ideally each stage builds on the previous knowledge and understanding, but they could also be undertaken independently of each other. These activities use simple techniques and methods which could be applied to other areas of your maths curriculum.

Aim of the activity:

To practise knowledge of number and place value by using natural materials. This can range from basic counting to finding unknown values in algebra further up the school.

Equipment:

- a large space with a hard surface where children can work in groups together;
- a range of natural materials such as sticks, leaves, acorns, berries, etc. (always check that you use materials that are safe for use with the pupils you are working with);
- chalk.

Description of the activities:

For each activity you will need a supply of natural materials such as sticks, leaves, cones, acorns, petals, etc. These could be collected by the children during the first couple of minutes of the lesson time, allowing them to have some physical movement before their focused activity. Alternatively, collect these in advance and have them ready for use in your maths lessons.

The techniques will be similar to those adopted in the classroom, but the use of the natural materials and the less formal space will engage with some pupils more. The use of a variety of concrete resources will help pupils to grasp concepts in a physical way and give them another method for solving number problems. They may also be more open to challenges and exploring their learning further in the outdoor environment.

Lower-level activities:

Counting

Anything that you do in the classroom with counters can be done outside with natural items such as leaves. Ask the children to count out a particular number of items for you to demonstrate their knowledge that one number counted correlates to one item.

Doubling

Ask the children to work in pairs. Initially get each child to pick up a single leaf each and then count how many they have in total if they put them together in their pair. Explain that having the same amount twice (multiplying the original number by two) is called doubling. Next, ask the children to each pick up two leaves and see what double two is. Work through different one-digit numbers, each time getting them to repeat the doubling facts, for example double 3 is 6, double 4 is 8. This works particularly well if you use crisp, dry, autumn leaves and allow the children to throw the leaves up in the air once they have found the doubling fact.

Number bonds

When exploring number bonds to 10, ask your pupils to collect 10 items and have them in front of them. Get them to check that they definitely have 10 items again before starting the activity. Draw a vertical line with chalk or use a stick so that they have two separate areas in front of them. Get them to place some of their items one side and the rest on the other. Encourage them to count the objects and write with chalk, or tell you how many are on each side and therefore what combinations of numbers add up to 10 in total. Encourage them to experiment with different combinations and turn these findings into number sentences written in chalk.

Middle-level activities:

Counting in 2s, 3s and 5s

There are objects that can be found in nature that can help with counting in groups of numbers and therefore multiplication facts. Challenge the children to find items that have groups of features, for example sycamore seeds that have two wings each, clovers that have three leaves, horse chestnut leaves that have five lobes on each leaf. By collecting a number of these, the children can then practise counting in their tables and check for accuracy using the concrete objects in front of them. If your school grounds do not have the species needed you could collect these before the lesson and bring them in, or simply use single resources placed in groups together for the same activity, for example the children count out and place the acorns into groups of five, then use these groups to help them count their five times tables.

Place-value representation

As your pupils start to work with larger numbers, it is important that they fully understand place value and the importance of the placement of each digit. Start by asking the children to collect a large pile of sticks and a large pile of leaves. Give the children a two-digit number and recap how to partition this into 10s and 1s. Ask them to use the sticks to represent how many 10s are in the given number and use the leaves as the 1s. Give the children a variety of two-digit numbers that they can partition and represent using their sticks and leaves. In pairs, ask them to give each other a number that can be shown and also written in chalk to show they fully understand the concept.

Challenge them by giving them a three-digit number – what natural object could they use to represent the 100s part of the number? Each time, ask them to write the number down in chalk and also partition and represent it using their natural materials.

Addition and subtraction number sentences

Once your pupils have become used to using the natural materials as dienes for partitioning, they can use these resources to help them to solve addition and subtraction problems. Start by giving them an addition problem to solve but ask them to partition and represent the numbers in the problem first before solving it. Explain that now they have broken down the numbers it will be easier to count how many 1s there are all together and how many 10s there are. Start with problems that do not cross the 10 (for example 34 + 23 or 41 + 48) and move on to more complex problems, just as you would in the classroom.

Use the same method to practise subtraction number sentences using the natural materials as dienes, in an outdoor space.

Higher-level activities:

Missing numbers

Natural objects can be used to represent numbers and encourage children to solve problems using the inverse of operations. Write out an example number sentence on the playground for your pupils to discuss in groups, for example 25 + a pinecone = 68.

Ask them to suggest how they could solve this and work out what the value of the pinecone is in this example. Once discussed and solved, give them some further problems, before letting them explore and challenge each other in groups. Can they use any other operations?

Natural equations

In a similar way to finding the missing numbers, this activity challenges pupils by giving values to items that they then must manipulate to create correct number sentences. See the example in Table 10.1.

Table 10.1

A leaf = 1	Use any operation that you want, to create a number sentence with the answers below:
A stick = 5	6, 13, 14, 25, 82, 84, 120
A stone = 7	Can you make up any more problems?
A seed = 10	
An acorn = 12	

Chalk can be used to write in the functions and the answers. Challenge the children by giving them answers that may or may not be possible and ask them to prove which can be done and which can't. Alternatively, give them some completed number sentences to check if they are correct or not.

All this missing number work is a great foundation for written algebra and understanding that symbols can be used as an unknown number.

Progression and extensions:

All of these activities can be followed as a progression of skills or used independently. If you are starting with one of the middle- or higher-level activities, spend some time recapping and ensuring your pupils are familiar with any necessary concepts before they get started.

Allow access to chalk and natural materials during break and lunchtimes and encourage the children to create their own number sentences or games using number, for example if they are playing a game in which they win points, can they show how many points they have won using natural items? Can they set each other challenges or problems to solve?

Adaptations:

Each of these activities can be adapted and tailored to suit the needs of your class and the number work that they are covering. For example, the number bonds activity can be delivered for number bonds to 20 instead or use 10s and 1 representations as shown in the place-value activity to explore larger number bonds such as 50, 100 or 1000.

MATHS AND NUMERACY ACTIVITIES CAN ALSO BE FOUND WITHIN THE FOLLOWING THEMES:

- Grow, cook, eat, celebrate – measuring the growing area, costs to grow versus cost in the shops, air miles, success of the harvest, volume of production, success of different crops over the year;
- Dig for Victory – rationing.

11
Science

INTRODUCING SCIENCE OUTDOORS

Many of the topics you teach in science are based on what happens outdoors. This is not just the biology of plants and animals but also the physics of forces and light and shade, the chemistry of what makes plants grow well, and much more.

The outside environment brings learning to life and provides the space for pupils to learn on a larger scale, create some noise and be more actively engaged. How much more memorable is it to learn about the parts of an insect or plant by seeing it outside in its natural habitat than reading about it in a book or watching it on a screen?

There are elements of the science curriculum that just can't be experienced inside. Identifying your local trees and wildflowers is better if done in the real world. Working with light and shadows can be easier outside too – as long as the sun is shining! Going outside at different times of the day and marking where the shadows are on the ground helps pupils to understand how the sun appears to move in the sky much more than just being told that this happens.

Whilst you can grow some plants on the windowsill – we have all grown cress haven't we – is it not more interesting to watch potatoes grow outside, harvest them, then cook and eat them yourselves? The time it takes for plants to grow is a valuable lesson for your pupils. They may not see much difference in some of the older trees in their grounds but they will see changes as courgettes and runner beans develop in their growing area.

Take a look at what you are teaching in science, consider cross-curricula themes too and you will soon find many opportunities to take your pupils outdoors.

Parachutes away!

Subject area: Science

Key focus: Forces

Also
- working scientifically
- weather – the wind

Level: Medium

Previous learning required:

Discuss what is meant by forces and how they can work in different directions, including gravity.
Talk about the fact that, even though we can't see the air, it is all around us and we can feel how it moves on a windy day.

Aim of the activity:

To understand how air resistance acts to slow down the motion of an object as it falls to the ground due to gravity.

Equipment:

- a range of pieces of material, plastic bags, etc.;
- string;
- light weights to act as the 'person' using each parachute;
- for adaptations – large sheets of card, small parachutes and cords to pull them along with.

Description of the activity:

Either prepare before the lesson, or get your pupils to prepare, a range of squares of different materials – mostly at least 20cm square. Make some larger than this and you can add some smaller ones too.

You also need four lengths of twine or string at least 20cm long for each parachute. These are tied to each corner of the squares.

A weight is then tied to the bottom of the four pieces of string – this needs to be heavy enough to make sure the parachute floats downwards but not too heavy for the size of the parachute. Test out a couple of options first before trying with your pupils – small world figures can sometimes be suitable but will depend on the size of the parachute.

Go outside and find a spot that is high up – up a few steps for example – so that there is space for the parachute to open up and for the parachutist to float down. Hold the parachute in the middle with the weight below then let it fall down to the ground. Compare how fast objects fall with and without parachutes.

What you are observing is gravity pulling the 'parachutist' down towards the ground and air resistance acting upwards on the parachute against gravity to slow the motion down. The greater the air resistance the greater the impact on the downward motion – which means that generally the larger the parachute the bigger the impact observed.

Your pupils may also observe the flight path veering off from straight down – this is the effect of the wind catching the parachute and moving it sideways.

Progressions and extensions:

Try out different sizes of parachute, different weights, different materials, the length of the string and different heights. What differences are observed and why do your pupils think this might be?

You can time the length of flight for the different options and compare this using graphs to analyse the data collected.

Adaptations:

Ask your pupils to feel the resistant force produced by the air by walking, running or wheeling along either with a large sheet of card in front of them or by pulling a parachute along behind them. You cannot see the air but you can feel that it is there! The larger the object catching the wind, the greater resistance they will feel.

Creating a compass

Subject area: Science

Key focus: Science - Forces - magnetism

Also
- geography – compass points

Level: Medium

Previous learning required:

Introduction to magnetism.
 Introduction to the concept of the magnetic north and using a compass.

Aim of the activity:

To make your own compass and embed an understanding of magnetism.

Equipment

- paper clips and a selection of items not suitable for making a compass with, such as pieces of plastic, dead matchsticks, pieces of magnetic material that are too big to float on a leaf, etc.;
- water and containers;
- leaves for the experiment, which can be collected by the pupils;
- manufactured compasses.

Description of the activity:

In this activity pupils are going to make their own compasses from a paper clip and a leaf. This is quite fiddly and needs good dexterity.

Introduce the concept of the compass – something that points to the magnetic north. These days your pupils may only have seen a compass on a mobile phone, so show them a physical compass too and let them see how this works. Explain that they are going to make their own compasses and this means they need something they can turn into a magnet. They will also need something that is not too big and that can float when placed on a leaf.

Each pupil or group has a container which they fill with water – use wide containers to give the leaves space to rotate in. They then collect a selection of leaves from around the grounds and see which float easily and freely in their container.

The next task is to choose the object they are to make into a magnet. Allow them to test a range of objects to find ones that are both magnetic and can float on the leaf. Paper clips are perfect for this.

Pupils should unfold their paper clips as much as they can. Hold the paper clip at one end and stroke the other end with a magnet in one direction twenty or so times. This will make the atoms in the paper clip line up in one direction, making it magnetic.

Your pupils then carefully lay their paper clip on the leaf and watch it slowly rotate until it is pointing north to south. They can check this by looking at a manufactured compass. They will need to be gentle, or else the leaf will sink, and be patient, as the turn can be very slow.

You can also use the original magnet to move the paper clip around on the water – move it a little way, remove the magnet and watch it turn back.

Progressions and extensions:

You can use a disc of cork and a chunky needle to make a compass too. Cut the cork down to about 1cm thick, magnetise the needle and carefully poke it through the cork horizontally so that when it floats, the needle points along the north–south axis. Check which end is north by testing out the new compass alongside a manufactured compass, then mark this on the cork along with the other main compass points.

Adaptations:

If dexterity is limited, provide pupils with an already homemade cork compass to test instead.

Why won't it move?

Subject area: Science

Key focus: Forces – friction

Also
- working scientifically

Level: High

Previous learning required:

Some work on forces including pushing and pulling.

Aim of the activity:

To develop an understanding of how the roughness of surfaces affects the amount of friction.

Equipment

- man-made slopes, e.g. a slide, hardboard, planks of wood;
- recycled bubble wrap or similar material with a textured surface on one side and smooth on the other;
- sticky tape;
- boxes with weights in;
- clipboards and pencils or whiteboards and markers.

Aim of the activity:

To see how friction is greater when surfaces are rougher.

Description of the activity:

Pupils start by finding out if their object will slide down their slope with a small push – just to get it going. They repeat the exercise but with the following modifications:

- Tape the bubble wrap bumpy-side-up onto their slope and add bubble wrap to the bottom of the box – bumpy side down. This means that both bumpy sides are facing each other.
- Change the bubble wrap on the slope so that the smooth side is uppermost.
- Then have the smooth side of the bubble wrap on the underside of the box and also on the top of the slope, i.e. smooth side to smooth side.

This exercise is all about the frictional force between the base of the object and the surface that it is sliding down. The rougher the surfaces the more friction is produced, which slows down movement, or even stops it. It is very clear to see how bumpy the bubble wrap is on one side and how smooth on the other. When both contact sides are bumpy it will be very hard to move the box, when they are both smooth it will be much easier.

Discuss with the class situations where you need friction – your shoes, for example, or where you need as little friction as possible – such as a water slide! Water is used here as a lubricant and helps reduce the friction, while making it easier to slide.

Progressions and extensions:

Change the angle of the slope in each situation and find the point where the box will move. Measure the angle to the ground and plot the results on a graph.

Make modifications by also changing the weights in the box and repeating the exercise above. Create new graphs to see the impact of the change in weight on how easily the box moves.

Adaptations:

If you have a slope down a hill this can be a fun activity to do – where your pupils can get very wet! They will therefore need to wear suitable clothing.

First, pupils should try to see how easy it is to move down the hill by just sitting on it and trying to slide – not rolling.

Then spread out tarpaulins down the slope and repeat the exercise (make sure there is nothing sticking out that could injure participants). Depending on the slope, you might get some movement, but when you flow water down the slope (and you need to keep it going for each attempt) the distance pupils will travel will be a lot further.

What's this made of?

Subject area: Science

Key focus: Materials

Also
- learning about the uses and properties of different materials found in the school grounds
- identifying things that are living, have been living or have never lived

Level: Low

Previous learning required:

To understand that different materials have different properties.

Aim of the activity:

To investigate the different properties and uses of materials found in the school grounds.

Equipment:

- clipboards, paper and pencils;
- a chart on which to fill in the name of an object, the material it is made from and why it is good for this purpose.

Description of the activity:

Start with everyone together investigating a couple of items found in the grounds – such as the asphalt, seats or fences. Prompt discussions by asking the following questions:

- What is the name of this feature?
- Do you know what it is made of? (This can be at quite a basic level, for example asphalt, wood, metal.)
- Was the thing that it was made from ever living? If so what was it like when it was alive?
- Why do you think it has been chosen for this function? What are the properties that make it good for this?
    - Is it hard or soft?
    - Does it move or stay still?
    - Do you think it ever moved or could be moved?
    - Is it waterproof? What happens to it when it rains?
    - What colour is it? Is this the natural colour or has it been painted?
    - Can you put something in it or on it (including a person!)?
    - Does it change something else by being there, for example the temperature, how people behave?
    - Could it have been made out of something else?

When you have looked at one or two items, send your pupils off to find more things in their grounds to look at and ask some of these questions, but also encourage pupils to devise their own additional ones. Review everyone's findings at the end.

The types of features you could look at include:

- surfaces:
    - grass
    - asphalt
    - safety surface.

- boundaries:
  - fences
  - walls
  - hedges.
- equipment in a growing area:
  - polytunnel or greenhouse
  - compost bin
  - planter or raised bed.
- furniture and other features:
  - seating
  - playground equipment
  - storage containers.

Progression and extensions:

You could mark these features on a map of the school grounds so that your pupils know which items you would like them to look at. They can always add their own too.

This could lead on to a project to add a new feature to the school grounds such as new seating or a greenhouse or polytunnel.

Adaptations:

If you have limited features in your grounds, make a visit to a park or other public open space within walking distance.

Where's the water gone?

Subject area: Science

Key focus: States of matter

Also
- the water cycle
- working scientifically
- changes in state
- evaporation

Level: Medium

Previous learning required:

Introduction to the water cycle and the process of evaporation.

Aim of the activity:

To develop an understanding of the water cycle and how evaporation fits into this.

Equipment:

- chalk;
- a camera;
- a tape measure or ruler;
- a sunny day;
- access to water;
- shallow plates or trays with a large surface area to put the water in;
- clipboards and pencils and a chart to write down the different measurements (breadth, length and depth of the puddle, its temperature and the temperature of the ground and air);

Take shallow containers that have a relatively large surface area outside to fill with water. The larger the surface area the more effect you will see as more water is evaporated. Measure the diameter and the depth of the water in the dish.

As the day progresses, the water will evaporate, so at regular intervals go outside and repeat the readings. Over the length of the day the water will evaporate and therefore reduce in size. The time taken to do this will depend on how sunny and warm it is – you will see most change on a sunny day in the summer. Link this to the water cycle and explain how the water on the ground evaporates and then condenses in the sky to form clouds, which will then turn to rain to create puddles that will evaporate, and so on.

Progressions and extensions:

Leave out your shallow dishes of water around the grounds in different places – some in the sun, some in the shade – and compare how long each takes to evaporate. You can also record the temperatures of the water, the ground and the air and see what impact this has too. To measure the water and air temperatures, use a mercury thermometer (1m above the ground to get the air temperature) and a temperature gun to measure the temperature of the ground.

Adaptations:

Paint can be dissolved in the water to colour it and make it easier to see. This also means that, as the water evaporates, a ring of paint is left behind so that pupils can see by how much the diameter of the water has shrunk.

Making rainbows

Subject area: Science

Key focus: Light and shadow

Also
- experimenting with sunlight and water

Level: Low

Previous learning required:

Understanding that we see rainbows when there is both sunlight and rain at the same time.
  The white light that we see is made up of the seven different colours of the rainbow – red, orange, yellow, green, blue, indigo and violet.
  To see a rainbow, you need to have the sunlight behind you and the water in front of you.

Aim of the activity:

To create a rainbow outside using water and the sun's light.

Equipment:

- a hose or watering can;
- water;
- a sunny day;
- a mirror, CD, water containers, light coloured paper or sheet (optional for 'Adaptations').

Description of the activity:

Explain that you are going to try creating your own rainbows using water and the sunlight. Ask the children when they have seen a rainbow before and remind them what colours they might see in them. Stand with the sun behind you and spray a hose of water or pour a watering can to make a fountain. Ask the children to look for a rainbow of light in the stream of water. Let your pupils have a go at making a rainbow themselves and be prepared that they may end up a little wet!

Progression and extensions:

Ask the children to identify the colours that they can see and spot other things in your grounds that match those colours. Challenge your pupils to make the largest or brightest rainbow that they can. Allow them to experiment with different angles of water and see if this makes a difference.

Adaptations:

If there is no sunshine available, experiment with using a torch or a different light source and see if you can make a rainbow. Here are some methods you could try:

- Hold up a transparent container of water so that the sunlight goes through it. See if you can spot a rainbow exiting the container and showing on the ground or on a piece of paper.
- Place a mirror or old CD partially submerged in a container of water. Angle it to face the sun and place some paper in between the water and the sunlight so you can see the rainbow.
- Hold a glass of water in front of a window that has sunlight passing through it. Hold some paper underneath the glass and see if you can spot a rainbow.

Could an animal live here?

Subject area: Science

Key focus: Living things and their habitats

Also
- scientific enquiry

Level: Low

Previous learning required:

An introduction to the needs of animals to survive, i.e. air, water, shelter and food.

Aim of the activity:

To find out if animals can live in our school grounds.

Equipment:

- none needed – but pupils could take out clipboards, paper and pencils, or whiteboards and markers.

Description of the activity:

Talk about the different things animals need to live, relating this also to humans:

- air to breathe;
- water to drink;
- food to eat;
- shelter to keep them safe and warm.

Discuss whether they think they have all these things in their school grounds. There will be air but what about water, food and shelter? You could talk about pollution here and how even the air we breathe can be limited in quality.

Talk about different animals that could live in your school grounds. Some of these are very small, such as insects and worms – these might eat grass or leaves and only need small amounts of water and a small place to shelter in, which might include living underground. Some are bigger and might eat the insects and worms and need more water to drink. This includes birds and hedgehogs. Some will be even bigger, such as foxes, which might visit some school grounds – probably when your pupils are not around. The bigger the animal the more food and water they need and the bigger the shelter or habitat they live in.

Go outside and take a tour of your grounds to discover if you have all the things you need for animals to live there.

Start in locations where you know animals live, such as trees, shrubs and grass. Investigate what makes them good places to live. Where might water gather when it rains, what might make good food and where can animals shelter? Can you spot any insects or birds in your trees? You can get an idea of the insects living in your tree by holding a sheet underneath and shaking some of the branches to see what falls out.

Do you have a pond? If so you probably know that lots of animals live in or next to it. There is water, there is food and there is shelter. But how do the animals that live in the pond breathe? Discuss how some animals, such as fish and tadpoles, have gills that allow them to breathe underwater.

Areas of just asphalt and brick or stone might at first seem to have nothing for animals to live on, but look again. Often water gathers in a dip in a rock or in a puddle on the playground. You may also find grass or other plants growing in crevices or corners, this can provide both food and shelter. It is likely that the shelter in these areas is not very big so any animals that live in this part of the grounds are going to be very small, such as insects. But remember these are important, as birds and other larger animals need these to feed on.

Progressions and extensions:

Investigate which animals live in your grounds or come to visit. Several wildlife organisations run community or school surveys and will supply you with all the information and resources you need to both undertake a survey, such as the UK Pollinator Monitoring Scheme (PoMS). Here are a few surveys to get you started:

- the Big Schools' Birdwatch run by the RSPB;
- the Big Butterfly Count run by Butterfly Conservation;
- Buglife has a range of surveys you can undertake for beetles and bugs;
- the X-Polli:Nation project has survey resources for pollinating insects;
- BeeWalk is a monitoring scheme run by the Bumblebee Conservation Trust.

If there is an animal you are interested in you will probably find a survey you can help with, so search the internet for national and local surveys. Including the term 'BioBlitz' in your search will also lead you to wildlife surveys.

Adaptations:

If you don't have many habitats or sources of water in your grounds but would like to see more wildlife, think about how you can help. Consider keeping areas of grass long, growing different flowering plants (including in pots), add some water and maybe make some habitats such as a bug hotel or bird boxes. (If you make habitats remember to clean them out on a regular basis to keep them disease free.)

Wildlife champions

Subject area: Science

Key focus: Living things and their habitats

Level: High

Previous learning required:

A tour of your school grounds to see if you can spot any wildlife or wildlife habitats.

Aim of the activity:

To learn about and from people and organisations who work in conservation in your area.

Equipment:

- clipboards, paper and pencils, or whiteboards and markers;
- access to the internet or other sources of information about wildlife organisations that work in your area.

Description of the activity:

You may already work with a local conservation group, but if you don't, the first part of this activity is to find out who there is in your area. There will be a range of wildlife and conservation organisations that are based in your area, from local volunteer groups to charities who employ staff, often including education staff who may be able to come into your school. Some organisations will have programmes that allow staff to visit schools without a cost, others may have to charge, so chat with them to find out what they can offer you and your pupils. Make sure both you and they know what to expect.

It is worth checking this out before asking pupils to research local groups so that you are sure someone will be able to come in.

Some of the national organisations who might have staff locally include:

- Learning through Landscapes;
- The Wildlife Trusts;
- RSPB (Royal Society for the Protection of Birds);
- TCV (The Conservation Volunteers);
- FSC (Field Studies Council);
- The Wildfowl and Wetland Trust;
- Butterfly Conservation Trust;
- Buglife;
- The Bumblebee Conservation Trust;
- Froglife;
- The Amphibian and Reptile Conservation Trust;
- Groundwork.

Invite them in to talk with your pupils about their organisation or a specific wildlife or conservation topic that you are studying. Start with your pupils giving them a tour around your site so that your 'expert' gets an idea of what your grounds are like. Before the visit, discuss with your pupils what they are going to say on the tour and what questions they would like to ask the expert so that you make the most of the visit.

Progression and extensions:

The wildlife organisation may be able to help you improve your school grounds for wildlife too. If this is the case see if they can work *with* your pupils on the following:

- learning about the wildlife that lives in the area;
- surveying your grounds to find out what lives there now;
- finding out what habitats and food different creatures need throughout their life cycles in order to thrive;
- helping pupils to plan changes to your grounds to make them more wildlife-friendly;
- helping pupils and the wider school community to make those changes;
- learning about how to care for your grounds and maintain them for the benefit of wildlife.

Adaptations:

Even if your grounds are very barren you will have some wildlife on site, but why not find out what other areas there are locally that you can walk to, or make an extended visit to, that have more wildlife for your pupils to see? Your local wildlife organisation may well have a site you can visit with your pupils.

Using my senses

Subject area: Science

Key focus: Animals, including humans

Also
- descriptive writing
- using maps (for the progression)
- art and design – mark making

Level: Low

Previous learning required:

An introduction to the five key senses: sight, smell, hearing, taste and touch.

Aim of the activity:

To make discoveries in the school grounds using your five key senses.

Equipment:

- clipboards, paper and pencils, or whiteboards and markers;
- simple maps of the school grounds (for the progression).

Description of the activity:

In this activity your pupils will see what they can find out about their school grounds using their five key senses: sight, smell, hearing, taste and touch.

As you brief your class at the start of the lesson, discuss the different activities you are going to do and get them to consider how they need to be more careful doing some things. For example, if they are going to taste something they need to know it is safe to eat – that might mean only eating things that you give them to taste. If they shut their eyes, then it is best if they stay still or be guided by a friend.

For the first activity they are going to listen to what they can *hear* around them.

Each sits quietly in a space and shuts their eyes so that they really concentrate on the sounds only. As they hear something, they should make a mark on their paper that 'looks' like the sound. Talk with them about how they might do this. What might the rumbling sound of traffic look like – maybe a long stretched out wiggly line? What might a bird's song sound like – maybe short, pointy marks on the page? There are no right or wrong marks or symbols.

Secondly your class is going to focus on *touch*. This might involve your pupils walking along different surfaces and describing what it feels like under their feet or rubbing their hands along different surfaces. Ask them to record words that describe what they are feeling, for example spongy, soft, sharp, tickly.

Next it is *taste*. If you are growing food or vegetables in your grounds then you have something you can use – you may even decide to cook it. Otherwise, you may want to think about what snacks your pupils eat at break times or food they eat outdoors in the grounds, such as marshmallows toasted over the fire or a celebration meal to mark a festival.

Then we visit *smell*. In an urban area this might include the smell of pollution, which could lead on to discussions about what it is created by and how it can affect health. Even in the smallest of school grounds you can grow some plants. Herbs are easy to grow in pots and planters and produce wonderful aromas. This might lead on to discussions about how you use herbs in cooking, which you might then try out.

Finally, we move onto *sight*. Ask your pupils to take a look around the grounds they have been exploring with their other senses. Are there things now they see that they might have missed if they hadn't 'looked' at them in other ways? Choose something they discovered with one of their other senses as a subject for a drawing.

Progression and extensions:

This activity can lead on to map making of your grounds. Instead of just the things they can see, add on the descriptions or images of the things they heard, felt, tasted and touched.

Adaptations:

Instead of using your whole school grounds, divide your class up to undertake sensory surveys of different parts of the grounds. When you finish, compare the different sensory experiences each group discovered and discuss why they might be different.

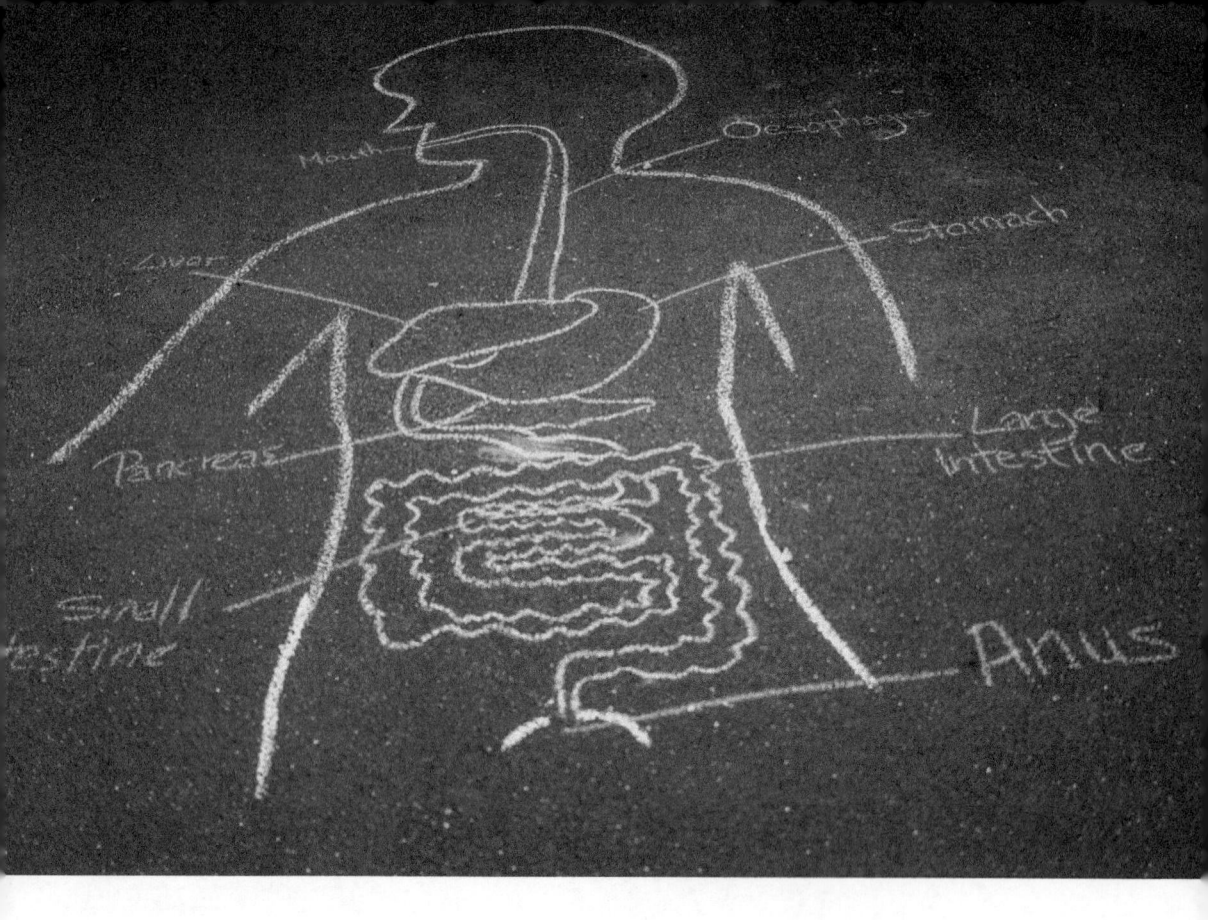

Walking the digestive system

Subject area: Science

Key focus: Animals, including humans

Also
- understanding the journey of food through the digestive system

Level: Medium

Previous learning required:

Knowing that the digestive system is a series of organs that allow your body to get the nutrients and energy that it needs from your food.

The digestive system also helps the body to remove any waste products.

Aim of the activity:

To create and identify the key parts of the digestive system and be able to show the journey of food through the body.

Equipment:

- a large open space;
- a variety of loose parts or sports equipment;
- chalk, whiteboards or post-it notes to label the parts of the digestive system (optional);
- pictures of the diagram of the digestive system (optional).

Description of the activity:

Split the class into small groups and remind them of the work they have already done around the digestive system. Explain that you are going to demonstrate the different parts of the digestive system by making a large diagram that shows the parts in order as a route through the body. Ensure each group has access to plenty of loose parts materials and enough space to create their diagram. If this activity is early in the topic, you may wish to give the groups a printed copy of the digestive system, or have one pegged up outside for them to look at and refer to if needed.

Key parts of the system for your pupils to show are:

- the mouth;
- oesophagus;
- stomach;
- liver;
- small intestine;
- large intestine;
- anus.

Once they have created their diagram, encourage your pupils to walk through the system, describing what is taking place at each stage of the digestive process. Exiting out the end of the system always causes some excitement and laughter!

Progression and extensions:

For some higher-level pupils, you could challenge them to add further details to their diagram, such as the epiglottis, pharynx, gallbladder, pancreas and rectum.

As a fun game, once the diagrams have been completed you could host a quiz or ask each team to quiz each other about the different organs. Names of organs could be given and your pupils run and stand in or on that organ. As a further progression, extended questions could be asked, such as what part of the body produces saliva or what is the longest organ in the digestive system?

Adaptations:

This activity could be completed as a revision exercise to demonstrate your pupils' knowledge at the end of the topic or to embed the learning around the digestive system. You could even ask them to complete a diagram as a test to see how much they can remember a few weeks after the unit of work.

The same method could be used for other biological systems that your pupils need to learn, such as the circulatory system. Or why not use sticks to create and label the bones of the human skeleton?

Understanding how sound can change in both volume and pitch

Subject area: Science

THREE PROGRESSIVE ACTIVITIES

Key focus: Sound

Also
- working scientifically
- scientific enquiry

Level: Progressive activities – medium (x 2) and high

Previous learning required:

For the first activity an introduction to sound, vibrations and sound waves. All the activities progress from each other.

Aim of the activity:

To use practical activities to help understand how sound can be created and how this changes over distance travelled and in pitch.

Equipment:

- see each individual activity.

Medium-level, first activity: how well does sound travel?

Aim of the activity:

To investigate if the volume of sound is reduced over a distance.

Equipment:

- something to make a consistent sound with, such as simple musical instruments, a dustbin lid and large stone dropped from a specific height or a sound recording;
- long measuring tape(s) or a measuring wheel;.
- one or more type of decibel app.

Description of the activity:

The aim of this activity is for pupils to set up an investigation to see how well sound travels over a distance. We are doing this outside as it provides greater distances to work with and therefore more changes in levels to be observed and more opportunities to be noisy without disturbing others!

Pupils should start by creating their hypothesis. What do they think will happen when they listen to sound over different distances?

They can then start to consider how they might carry out their experiment outside, the equipment needed, their methodology and what they are going to observe and record. What sounds will they create and listen to? How can they make sure it is always the same volume (try dropping a large stone from the same height onto a saucepan or play a recorded sound, for example)? What equipment will they need? Where is the best place to do this experiment? How will they record the different volume levels? Decibel apps have different levels of accuracy (you could compare these as part of the experiment) but they do give a good idea of when things are comparatively louder or quieter. Pupils can also listen alongside using the app – how far do they go before they can't hear one of the sounds?

Do you have the space to run several tests at the same time or will you have to work on one experiment at a time?

How will the results be recorded? How can you be sure your results are accurate, especially not knowing how accurate the apps might be? Perhaps by taking more readings and averaging out the results to reduce error. Collect the distance at which the volumes were measured together with the measurement from the app.

Once the data is gathered it can be analysed and graphs drawn to show how the volume of the sound diminished over distance.

Progression and extensions:

Do pupils think it will matter if there are objects between them and the source of the sound? Does is matter what that object is made of – do some materials absorb the sound better than others? Does it make a difference if the person making the sound or the person listening to it is behind an object such as a tree or a wall?

Adaptations:

If you have limited space or will be disturbing others by making a noise outside try making quieter sounds. These differences may not show so well on the app so instead see how far pupils have to move away from the sound before they can't hear it.

Medium-level, second activity: is the pitch of sound higher or lower?

Aim of the activity:

To see how the length of an 'instrument' affects the pitch of sound.

Equipment:

Depending on availability you could use any of the following:

- tubes or pipes of different lengths – you may have 'Boomwhackers' but plastic piping works as well;

AND/OR

- glass bottles filled with different amounts of water – and a source of water such as a tap or watering can. Funnels can also be useful to make filling the bottles easier;

AND/OR

- instruments in your grounds such as large xylophone or chimes;

AND

- beaters with which to play your instruments;
- tape measures.

Description of the activity:

The aim of the activity is to see how the length of an instrument affects the pitch of the sound produced. The outdoors is a good place to do this activity as you can make more noise, more people can work spread out and so not disturb others' experiments, and you can use water to make your instruments without worrying about spillages!

Pupils should hypothesise about whether the sounds will be higher, lower or the same if they change the length or height of the instrument they are using. If you are using water in bottles then you are measuring the height of the water.

Provide pupils with the equipment available for the experiment so that they can decide on their methodology, the equipment needed and the observational recordings they are going to make. How will they record those findings?

Go outside to set up the experiment, spreading groups out so that they don't disturb each other.

They will find that the longer or taller the instrument, the lower the sound they produce when it is struck. This is because the wavelength produced is longer.

If you are using Boomwhackers they will have the different notes produced written on them. If this is the case you can measure the tubes and plot the pitch of the notes against the length of the tubes.

In all cases, pupils should note the different lengths or heights of each instrument and put them in order with the highest pitch on the right and the lowest on the left. Pupils will observe that they will be laid out in an ever-decreasing size as the notes get higher.

Progression and extensions:

Discover that doubling the length of the tube or height of the water changes the pitch of the note by an octave.

You can get apps that will tell you the note you are playing. These often need a constant note, so pupils may need to sing the note they hear from the instrument played to get a result.

Tune your instruments so that you have a scale of notes, then create and perform simple music.

Higher-level activity: slow motion sound

Aim of the activity:

To hear what happens to sound when it is slowed down.

Equipment:

A selection of items that you can make sounds with – enough for pupils to work in small groups. This could include some of the following:

- gravel and a metal trowel or spade to drop it onto;
- a watering can with a rose spout filled with water;
- railings, fencing or decking and a long, sturdy stick;
- a stack of flowerpots and a stick to knock them down with;
- a phone or tablet with a slo-mo function.

Description of the activity:

The aim of this activity is for pupils to discover the relationship between the frequency of a soundwave, its wavelength and the pitch of the sound produced.

Revise the learning that sound produces soundwaves and that soundwaves with a low frequency and longer wavelength produce low-pitched sounds whilst shorter soundwaves with a higher frequency produce high-pitched sounds.

In this activity pupils will record a variety of sounds using slo-mo recording.

Pupils explore a range of sounds outside. Working in small groups they use the slo-mo function on phones or tablets to record the different sounds. Check that the camera function or app they are using does play back the sound at a lower speed, some can play back the picture more slowly but keep the sound at the same pitch. They can watch and listen back in slow motion to the sounds of what they have recorded. They should choose two or three of their favourite sounds and also record these in real time.

Back in class play some of the slo-mo sounds (sounds only) to the class to see if they can work out how the sound was made. You can then show the video of the slo-mo and real-time recordings.

Discuss the difference between the recordings. Why did the slo-mo versions sound so low? This is because as you slow down the video so the sound gets slowed down and stretched. The soundwaves become longer and the frequency is reduced – therefore the sound is lower.

Progression and extensions:

Pupils model how sounds travel using their own movement. Start by getting them to stand or sit in a line where they can *just* reach the shoulders of the person in front of them.

The person at the back taps the shoulders of the person in front who, when feeling this, does the same to the person in front of them. Time how long it takes for the 'soundwave' to move down the row.

Repeat this with everyone being a little further apart, so that the line is stretched and your pupils have to move forward to reach the next person in the line. Time how long this takes.

This is like stretching the soundwave. If this was a soundwave, the sound would be at a lower pitch.

Adaptations:

Instead of small groups working on their own the whole group could work together with staff recording a range of sounds they make, such as singing or clapping.

SCIENCE ACTIVITIES CAN ALSO BE FOUND WITHIN THE FOLLOW THEMES:

- Grow, cook, eat, celebrate – living things, the seasons, requirements of plants to live, changing through cooking, temperature changes of fire;
- Dig for Victory – compare growing heritage seeds to modern varieties, learn about the parts of plants, draw root structures on raised beds;
- Pollination – researching the life cycles of pollinating insects, habitats and presenting findings;
- Seasonal change – life cycles and reproduction – plants and animals, interdependence, the movement of the moon.

12
Humanities

TEACHING HUMANITIES OUTDOORS

It is probably quite clear why geography lessons and activities should sometimes be taken outside – that is where landforms and the impact of man on the environment can be seen and where maps are used.

Our history is also very visible outdoors – buildings, trees and landscapes bridge the time between generations. Historically, many events took place outside whilst for many people much of their lives would have taken place outdoors. In order to discover more and make historical events more meaningful, consider taking your learning outdoors and bringing those times to life.

For many people, those with a faith and those with none, the outdoor environment brings peace, sustenance and comfort. It is a place in which we refresh mind, body and spirit and it is a place where we can contemplate big issues such as caring for the environment and the creatures that live there. It can also help us to address difficult topics such as death as we see changes around us across the seasons and over the years, or as we create places for reflection.

Many stories from religious texts are set outdoors, with key figures responding to the world and weather around them. Many festivals take place outdoors, whilst prayers across faiths often focus on creation and care for our world. Taking an assembly outside can also lead to a more memorable time together, whilst having more lessons and lesson activities outside may bring different responses to topics from your pupils than being indoors.

Outdoor spaces are also often more relaxed than indoor spaces, providing opportunities for staff and pupils to respond to each other in different ways. Working alongside someone, such as in the school growing area, can lead to discussions that might otherwise not have happened, sometimes allowing for deeper discussions or more informal conversations across a wide range of topics.

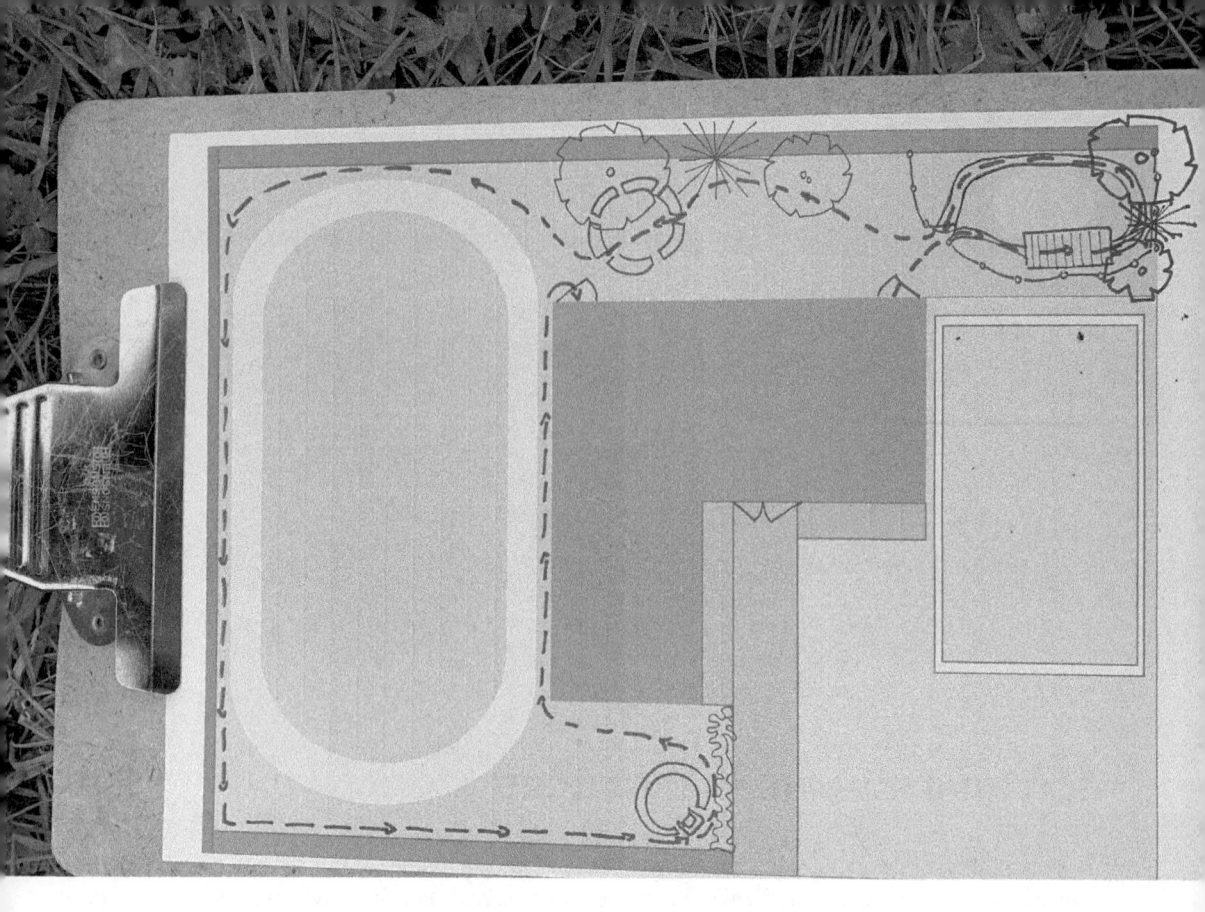

Follow that ...

Subject area: Geography

Key focus: Maps and navigation

Also
- using simple fieldwork and observational skills to study the geography of your school grounds and key human and physical features within it

Level: Low

Previous learning required:

Introduction to maps and how to identify locations or objects marked on them.

Aim of the activity:

To be able to locate positions on a map of the school grounds and to add information to that map.

Equipment:

Equipment needed for each small group:

- simple maps of the school grounds with different trails marked on each (one map per small group of pupils);
- clipboards, paper and pencils;
- coloured crayons;
- compasses and tape measures for the progression activity.

Description of the activity:

This activity is about following a pathway on a map in a space pupils know well and also recording a trail on a map.

Split the class into an even number of small groups (2–4 pupils in each), give each group a map with a trail marked on it and pair them up with a group with a different trail on it.

The first group have to follow their trail and the second group follow them (they can pretend to be stalking them and try not to be seen), marking down on their copy of the map where they think their partner group is going.

When the first group is finished, swap over so that the second group is now following a trail and the first group is marking this down on their maps.

When this has been done, compare the two sets of maps – how well did the groups both follow the maps and mark them down correctly?

Progression and extensions:

Instead of drawing the directions on the map, pupils could write and follow directions using a compass – for example 20 metres north followed by 15m east, then mark these on the map as they progress. Use compasses and tape measures for accuracy. They could also set their partner group a challenge and see how well they follow these instructions. Compare the two maps again at the end of the activity.

Adaptations:

The maps and instructions could be made easier or harder depending on the group. Instead of trails or compass points to move to, they could move between features in the ground, for example go to the storytelling chair first, then turn right and walk to the gate to the wildlife area.

The travelling fruit

Subject area: Geography

Key focus: Maps and navigation

Also
- using simple fieldwork and observational skills to study the geography of their school grounds and key human and physical features within it
- using digital mapping apps (adaptation for technology)

Level: Medium

Previous learning required:

Introductions to maps and how to identify locations or objects marked on them.

Aim of the activity:

To be able to locate positions on a map of the school grounds and to add information to that map.

Equipment:

- a selection of fruit and vegetables grown in the school grounds or brought in if you do not grow any. You will need something different for each group.

Equipment needed for each small group:

- simple maps of the school grounds;
- clipboards, paper and pencils;
- a coloured pen or crayon.

Description of the activity:

This activity is about mapping – using fruit and vegetables. Each is moved around the grounds by pupils, then searched for, found and mapped by others.

Pupils work in groups. Each group chooses, or is allocated, a fruit or vegetable – you will need something different for each group so they know which fruit or vegetable belongs to them. They should design a map symbol for their item and use this when marking the maps.

The first person in each group takes their piece of fruit or vegetable and places it in full sight somewhere in their school grounds. They should put it somewhere that it would not be expected to be seen so that there is no confusion with other fruit or vegetables outside. No one else in their group should see where it is put.

When the first person returns to their group, the second person sets off. When they find the item, they take a photograph of it and mark its location on the map of the school grounds with their chosen symbol. They then reposition the item somewhere else in the grounds for the next person to find.

This continues until everyone has had a go at finding the item and repositioning it – so when the last person has repositioned the fruit the first person has to find it so that everyone has a go at both placing and searching for the fruit.

On completion of the activity, print out the photographs and add them to the map where they were found. Mark the pathways the fruit and vegetables took on each individual map using the symbols designed by each group.

Progression and extensions:

The different pathways can be added to one map to see the different routes each group took. The groups can then work out how far each item has travelled by measuring the different pathways on the map and see how far their fruit or vegetable travelled compared with the others.

Adaptations:

Instead of drawing the maps you can use digital maps to 'place' your found fruit and vegetables. Add the photographs of the fruit in position at each location point.

What makes our school grounds special?

Subject area: Geography

Key focus: People and place

Also
- locating features on maps

Level: Low

Previous learning required:

None required.

Aim of the activity:

To explore the different elements of your school grounds and what makes them special.

Equipment:

- clipboards, paper and pencils;
- a map of the school grounds;
- cameras.

Description of the activity:

All school grounds are unique, so in this activity you will look at what makes your school grounds special. This can be a great activity to undertake as new pupils arrive in the school and get to know the grounds, or as a reflection on the elements they have grown to like over time.

Take a tour of your grounds with your pupils and look at the different spaces and features in your grounds. Ask your pupils about each space you visit. Here are some questions you could use:

- Do you think there are ways you are expected to behave in this space? Do you think it is a space to be quiet or to run around and be noisy?
- Do you choose to spend time in this space? Why is that – what can you do here? What features does it have that make you want to use it?
- What kind of materials are used in this space? Are they hard or soft, natural or man-made, bright and colourful or duller and greyish?
- How does this space make you feel?
- Do our grounds have lots of nature in them or are they just full of hard surfaces such as asphalt, brick and stone?
- Do we have any features in our grounds that make them special? This might be art, a piece of equipment or sports court, a water feature, the school building itself, a hedgerow or an area of trees.
- Are there features and spaces that have special functions – e.g. sports courts and pitches, the pond, a seating area? How do you know what that purpose is? What are the clues that tell you what happens there?
- Which are your favourite spaces in our grounds? Why have you chosen those spaces? What makes them good places to spend time in?
- How might you change this space to make it better?

Using maps of the grounds, pupils can colour in the different areas of the grounds in green for their favourite spaces, orange for those that are OK and red for spaces they don't really like. When this has been done, these maps can be compared and the class's favourite and least-favourite spaces can be found. This might be the starting point for a new school grounds development project!

Progression and extensions:

Consider what surrounds your grounds too. Are you in an urban setting or surrounded by countryside? Are there features that are specific to your location, such as mountains and hills or housing and factories?

Can you see these views from inside your grounds? Do they impact on the way the grounds feel?

Adaptations:

With some pupils you may find taking a toy outside to act as an intermediatory for your conversations can be helpful. Instead of asking a pupil what they like in their grounds, they can suggest where teddy might like to spend time or undertake a specific activity.

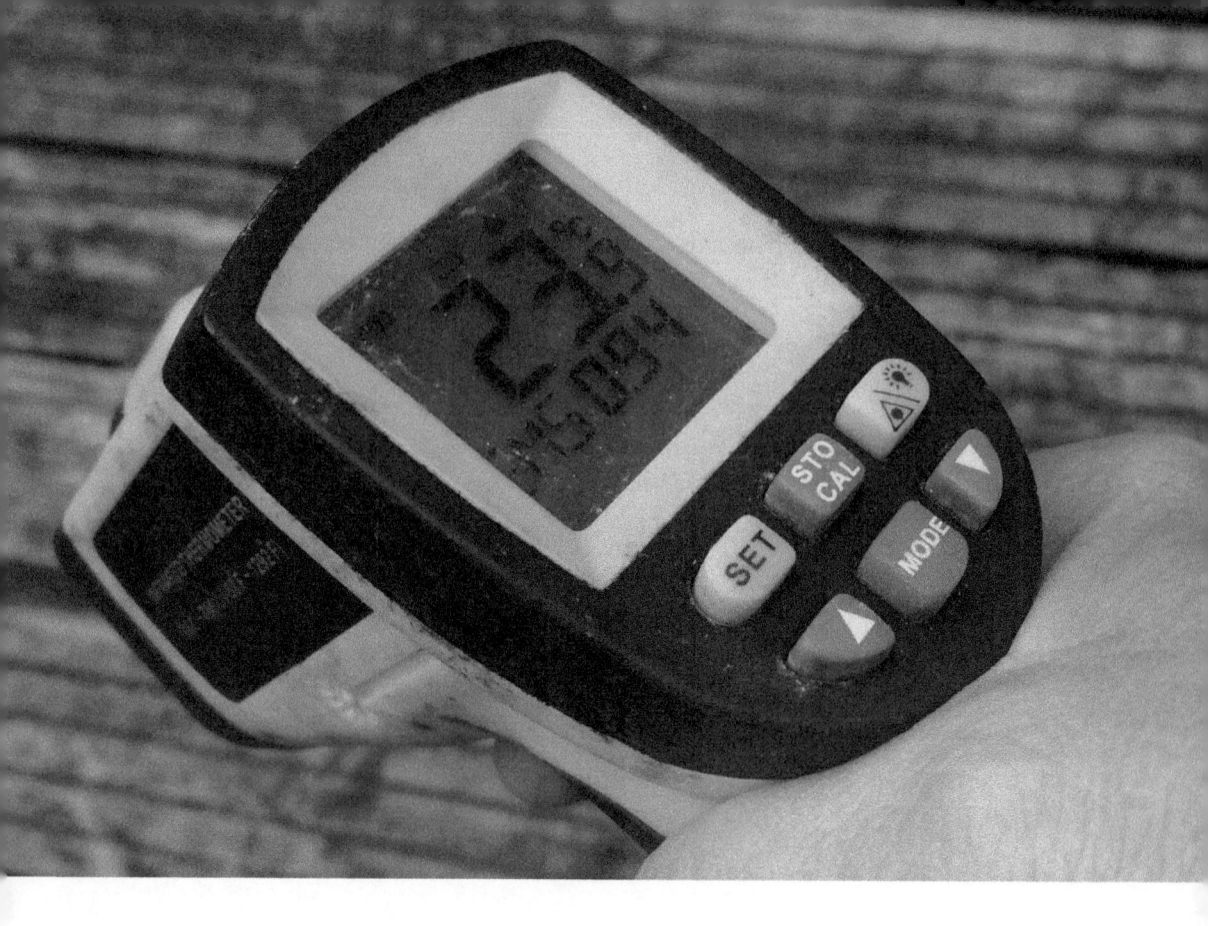

It's how hot?

Subject area: Geography

Key focus: People and place

Also
- interdependence
- science – scientific enquiry
- maths and science – gathering, displaying and analysing data

Level: High

Previous learning required:

Introduction as to how the changes humans make to the landscape have an impact on climate.

Aim of the activity:

To discover how different surfaces in the school grounds heat up on sunny days.

Equipment:

- heat guns;
- mercury thermometers taped to the top of 1m high sticks;
- clipboards, paper and pencils;
- temperature charts to complete – see description of the activity.

Description of the activity:

The changes we make to landscapes can make the impact of climate change worse, and the aim of this activity is to look at how hotter days can be made to feel even hotter by the type of surfacing we have on the ground.

Start by discussing the impact of climate change, that we are going to have hotter summers and wetter winters. This then has an impact on humans, on which plants can grow where and which animals can survive. Factors that will change the temperature we feel will include how much shade there is, the orientation and slope of the ground we are on (the longer it faces the sun in the middle of the day the hotter it will get), whilst the types of materials we use in the landscape can also make a difference to how hot it feels. Ask your pupils to predict which parts of their school grounds will get the hottest on a sunny day and why that might be.

In this activity your pupils measure the temperature of different surfaces with the heat gun and use a standard thermometer taped onto the top of a one metre stick to read the temperature of the air at a constant height above the surface. You will get the best results on a sunny day, even a cool one.

Your pupils will then complete the following table:

Table 12.1

Location or feature	What it is made of	Orientation and if on a slope	In direct sun or in the shade	Temperature at ground level	Temperature at 1m above the ground
Playground	Asphalt (Tarmac)	Faces north south, flat	In direct sun	$x°C$	$y°C$

Present the data on a graph and analyse it to discover which surfaces and air above them are the hottest and why that is. You will discover that man-made surfaces tend to be much hotter than those made of natural materials or shaded by plants. This has an impact on how hot we feel in a space.

Progressions and extensions:

Consider making changes to your grounds to make them cooler spaces in the summer. This might include creating shade by planting or hanging up tarpaulins or sheets or even changing the surfacing of part of your grounds.

Adaptations:

All school grounds will have different temperatures in different parts of the grounds. However, if your ground is all asphalt, consider bringing in some plants in pots so that you can see what the temperature is like with soil or vegetation as a surface.

Oldest and newest

Subject area: History

Key focus: Timelines and a sense of place

Level: Low

Previous learning required:

An introduction to how some things are older than others and how we can tell if something is old or new.

Aim of the activity:

To identify some of the oldest and newest things in your school grounds.

Equipment:

- clipboards, paper and pencils or whiteboards and markers;
- cameras.

Description of the activity:

Understanding the progression of time can sometimes be quite tricky – especially if you have only experienced a few years of life yourself. In this activity we investigate which features on the school site have been there for a long time and which are very new, and what clues you might see to help you make your decisions.

Before you go out on a tour of the grounds, discuss with your pupils what they will see when they go outdoors. How do they think they will be able to tell if something is very old or very new? Brainstorm a list of clues with them so that when they go outside they can decide what to photograph, draw or note down.

Is it easier to tell if something is old if it is alive? Trees that are older tend to be taller or wider, but a building doesn't grow once it has been built, for example.

What about asking older people whether the feature you are looking at was there when they were the pupils' age?

Things that have been outside for a long time can change because of the weather and through use. The wind, rain, sun and wear can all change things so that they don't look as bright or have as sharp edges as they did when they were first created.

Are there any dates on anything? Sometimes buildings have a date on them as to when they were opened.

When you return inside, talk about what you discovered and whether it was easy or difficult to tell if something was old or new. Are there other ways you can find out the age of different features? Some schools keep photographs from when the school was opened to the present day. Take a look at the photos over the years to see what has changed.

Progressions and extensions:

Look at old maps to see how things have changed in the grounds over the years. Ordnance Survey can help you find maps from different centuries showing what has been on your site before there was a school. Ideally you want to find a map from just before the school was built and one just after, so that your pupils can work out when it was created.

Adaptations:

If your school is very new, focus on what was on the site before there was a school. There might have been a different school, a field, housing or a factory. Why not invite older members of the community in to talk about what they remember of the area before the school was built?

History under the ground

Subject area: History

Key focus: Timelines and a sense of place

Level: Medium

Previous learning required:

An introduction to how things become 'buried' underground over time and how we can sometimes find things out about people and animals who have lived before us by digging into the ground.

Aim of the activity:

To be introduced to palaeontology or archaeology by 'discovering' items buried in your school grounds.

Equipment:

- clipboards, paper and pencils or whiteboards and markers;
- cameras (optional);
- trowels for digging;
- gloves;
- water and brushes to clean your finds;
- a sand pit or area of soil that can have something buried and dug up in.

Description of the activity:

Unless you are very lucky, if you dig into your school grounds you are unlikely to find anything of any historical interest (and if you do, call in your local archaeologist straight away). So, in order for your pupils to experience what it is like to discover something underground, you are going to have to put it there.

This is where the fun begins! You may like to hide some dinosaur bones or footprints, or some objects from an era you are studying, such as pieces of pottery, bottles or coins. You can make bones and footprints out of plaster of Paris or clay. If you want your pupils to find pottery, use something as simple as pieces of a clay flowerpot and decorate it in a style of the time you want it to represent.

A large sand pit, if you have one, is a great place to hide your finds – it is easy to dig into sand and keeps everyone relatively clean.

Alternatively, find a space in your grounds that is easy to dig and bury your items. Pupils can work in dig teams – digging, cleaning and recording by drawing and describing each of the items they find. They should always use gloves, and be careful when digging things up and cleaning them so that they don't break.

Discuss what you have found in the grounds. What do the objects you found tell us about the people who used the site before you?

Make sure you finish by explaining that you placed the items in the grounds so that they don't continue digging them up.

Progressions and extensions:

Bury your finds at different locations around the grounds and provide your pupils with a map of where to search for them. They will also need tape measures, canes and string for marking out where they are going to put the archaeology trenches.

If you have buried items relating to a specific period of history, you could also include an object that is clearly from another era for an odd-one-out challenge.

Adaptations:

If you don't have a sand pit you can replicate the experience by using sand in boxes – but make sure you use play sand not builders' sand, as this stains.

Our class timeline

Subject area: History

Key focus: Timelines and a sense of place

Level: High

Previous learning required:

Understanding how events happen over time.

Aim of the activity:

To create a class timeline in your school grounds.

Equipment:

- clipboards, paper and pencils;
- chalk;
- long measuring tapes;
- a wall, fence or washing line and something to pin up your timeline such as clothes pegs.

Description of the activity:

The aim of this activity is to create a timeline in your school grounds that marks important times in the life of your class. As you are only looking at 11 or 12 years the times can be quite spread out across the playground or along a wall, fence or washing line.

As a class, decide on the specific events you want to put on your timeline. Divide these into class events, personal events and national or international events.

Consider which class-related events you want to record. This could be when the class first started school and each person's birthday.

After this, research events that have happened in the class's lifetimes that will become history. What do they think will be the history of the future? How do they decide which events to add and which to leave out? This could include new technological or sporting events such as the Olympics and Paralympics, or the start of the pandemic.

Then take the class outside and find the longest straight line you can mark out in your grounds – use existing lines on the ground where you can, such as a netball court side line, a line of bricks in a wall (to save time and chalk), or fix up a washing line out of the way of everybody else. Measure the length of your line, then divide it by the number of years you are covering and mark these onto your line. You can then divide each year into 12 months and decide if you want to go right down to each day (you could prepare this before the lesson or use it as part of a maths exercise).

Start by marking the class events on the line, then your pupils can add in their own special days. You could add them in by chalking on the ground or create markers in class that can be added to the lines.

Finally, add the soon-to-be historical events. From here you will clearly see what has happened in the short lifetime of your pupils.

Progressions and extensions:

As well as adding the events from the lifetime of your class you could extend this to the lifetime of the school. If your school is brand new you could investigate what was on the site before. Add in local information and talk with parents and grandparents about what has happened in their lifetime.

You will also need to think about the scale of your timeline. The events you have spread out in your pupils' lifetime will become squashed up in comparison with other events, which will help them get a perspective of the passing of time.

Adaptations:

Consider other ways of displaying the information, such as securing a timeline onto a fence. You may even want to turn key events in the life of the school into a permanent mural or mosaic.

Building Bronze Age dens

Subject area: History

Key focus: Understanding how Bronze Age people lived

Also
- Experiencing history through building within a team

Level: Low

Previous learning required:

Some knowledge of everyday life in Bronze Age Britain, including village life and farming. Experience of tying basic knots will be useful.

Aim of the activity:

To explore how Bronze Age people made their homes with locally found materials and to work in a team to make a den which has similar features.

Equipment:

- pictures of Bronze Age roundhouses, either photos from outdoor museums, or school grounds (as in the image opposite) or artists' illustrations;
- den-building materials such as tarpaulins, cloth, rope, hazel poles, branches, cardboard and fixings. Poles already banged into the ground are a great starting point.

Description of the activity:

Study the pictures of roundhouses and discuss the following points: the materials Bronze Age people used and where they obtained them; what kinds of building techniques you think they may have used; the key external and internal features of a roundhouse and what kinds of things you might find inside. Next, ask pupils what they think a shelter or home needs to offer people. They may suggest things like a roof, or that it should provide space and security, be wind and waterproof, or warm.

In small groups, ask your pupils to think about the features they will include while building their dens, as they will be invited to give the rest of the group a guided tour later.

Groups who finish early can be encouraged to construct some outdoor community spaces for the village.

When all pupils have completed their dens, take a tour of the Bronze Age den village, with each group giving a guided tour focusing on any Bronze Age features they have incorporated. Finish up with ideas and a class vote on a name for the village they have created.

Progression and extensions:

- The building process and guided tours can be the basis for a persuasive writing exercise in which your pupils describe how they made their den (or a village of dens) and what Bronze Age features it had. Pupils could take photographs to illustrate their written pieces.
- Pupils will enjoy making things to go in their dens, such as whittling a wooden spoon from twigs using a potato peeler, or making some charcoal paint art.

Adaptations:

The same building activity can be done on a small-world scale, with pupils making mini-roundhouses from collected natural materials or from recycled materials.

Sensing a story

Subject area: Religious and moral education

Key focus: Learning stories from scriptural texts

Also
- language and literacy – listening and responding to a story

Level: Low

Previous learning required:

Listening to stories.

Aim of the activity:

To familiarise pupils with a scriptural text through storytelling using a variety of senses.

Equipment:

This will be different for each story told, so you will need:

- a selection of items that highlight or emphasise different aspects or parts of the story being told. For example, you might need some water if it rains in the story, or you might want seeds if it is about a farmer growing crops. If you, or your pupils, can collect these items from around your grounds that is even better.

Description of the activity:

Pupils sit in pairs as the teacher tells the story. They face each other and have a selection of items that they will be told to use throughout the story. One of the pair will be the giver, the other the receiver (sitting in two concentric circles with the storytellers in the middle works well). This activity works particularly well outside as there is more space to sit, you can find a quiet place to work, you can use water if it is in the story, and you may be able to collect resources from your own grounds.

The receiver has their eyes closed throughout the storytelling.

The giver has the items that will bring new sensory dimensions to the story.

As the story is read out the receiver holds their hands out in front of them – palms up – and the giver places or drops the sensory item for that part of the story into their hands. This might be a spray or droplets of water to represent rain, pebbles representing boulders, a breeze created to represent the wind.

Stories you could use in this activity:

- Creation stories;
- stories involving the seasons and plants growing;
- stories of journeys;
- parables and moral stories.

The receiver feels the items in their hands and is given time to do this before the story moves on. The additional sensory aspects to the storytelling will help to bring the story to life and help pupils to remember the stories.

Progression and extensions:

Pupils can find the sensory items themselves for the storytelling. They can either be told what to collect or be told the features of the story they want to enhance and choose items to match this. This could be done with a second story once they have the idea of how it works.

Alternatively, they can choose a story to tell the class and decide which items they want everyone to have to enhance their storytelling.

Adaptations:

This activity works well with children of a wide range of abilities and needs – especially as the receiver.

Exploring labyrinths

Subject area: Religious and moral education

Key focus: Exploring Christianity and other faiths

Also
- understanding what a labyrinth is
- creating a labyrinth pattern
- exploring mindfulness

Level: Low–high

Previous learning required:

This activity does not require any prior knowledge but might work as a companion to learning about prayer and meditation in a number of faiths.

Aim of the activity:

To develop an understanding of what labyrinths are and what different faiths use them for.

Equipment:

- chalk or rope;
- small loose parts such as shells, pebbles, etc.;
- search online for instructions on how to make a labyrinth;
- for a progression – verses from scripture, lines of poems, questions or photographs to be laid out around the labyrinth for pupils to focus on as they walk around;
- music to accompany the walking of the labyrinth.

Description of the activity:

Begin by exploring images of labyrinths, perhaps completing a mind map with the children to gauge their understanding of the concept. Explain that labyrinths have been part of human cultures for thousands of years, often serving a spiritual or meditative purpose. There are many different types, but the *classical labyrinth* usually consists of a single pathway that loops back and forth to form seven circuits, bounded by eight walls, that surround the centre. Start by making three-ringed labyrinths with groups of pupils; you can make a larger one together too. Labyrinths are different from mazes in that there is only one path. People walk along the path from one end to the other and pray, meditate or just spend time in peace and quiet.

Take your pupils outside. Split the children into small groups (3–4 is ideal). Next, ask them to spread out and create their own labyrinths using the instructions above. They can draw these with chalk, lay out ropes or even mark the path with stones or shells. Remind pupils that the paths should be clear and wide enough for a person to walk along. Give pupils enough time to complete their labyrinth patterns, then try them out in their small groups.

Once each group has created their labyrinth, they could rotate round each of the other groups. Remind pupils that the activity is to be peaceful and that the paths are a way of focusing and calming your thoughts. They should walk slowly round their labyrinths and spread out so they don't bump into each other.

Gather the children and help them reflect on the experience. Was it enjoyable? Did anyone feel calmer? Which labyrinths were the most interesting to walk around? Did the shape make a difference? Note their assessments on the mind map.

Progression and extensions:

Many cultures have used variations on the labyrinth over the centuries, including the Celts, the Mayans, the Greeks and Early Christians. This idea could complement a wider project in any of these subjects. Pupils may enjoy exploring the differences between labyrinths and mazes. There may be mazes and labyrinths in parks and historic gardens local to you, which would be good to visit and experience.

Adaptations:

The whole class could create a much larger labyrinth to share their learning with other year groups. This could be mown grass, made from excluding light from grass to create the path or painted onto the playground. You can then add different elements such as music being played as pupils walk around it, or verses, images or questions laid out at different points to consider as pupils walk the pathway.

You could also make much smaller labyrinths on walls or benches, where pupils follow the pathway with their fingers. If you have a quiet garden this could be a lovely addition.

HUMANITIES ACTIVITIES CAN ALSO BE FOUND WITHIN THE FOLLOWING THEMES:

- History appears in:
    - Dig for Victory – exploring why people had Dig for Victory gardens; consider tools and equipment; create interpretation signs; write and perform speeches to support the war-effort;
    - The Vikings have arrived;
    - What did the Vikings eat for breakfast?
    - Did they get on with their neighbours?
    - Would I feel at home in a Viking house?
    - Clothes, textiles and crafts;
    - Storytelling and writing;
    - Viking PE and games.
- Geography appears in:
    - Pollination – habitat mapping;
    - Seasonal change – climate and weather, how things change.
- Religious and moral education appears in:
    - Grow, cook, eat, celebrate – links with faith groups to mark festivals; grow food with links to faiths;
    - The Vikings have arrived – did they get on with their neighbours?
    - Seasonal change – rights of passage, festivals and events throughout the year.

13
The arts

TEACHING THE ARTS OUTDOORS

The outdoor environment provides the arts with many teaching opportunities that the indoor environment cannot. It gives us:

- more space;
- an ever-changing environment;
- nature to observe and be inspired by;
- natural materials to work with;
- a different backdrop and environment to work in.

Cicero is said to have written, 'Art is born of the observation and investigation of nature.' If we consider nature in its broadest sense to not only include living things but also the weather and climate, the air we breathe and how people respond to the world around them, then that resource to work from, in and with is endless.

Artists, composers, choreographers and playwrights across the centuries have been inspired by the outdoor environment. From representational art where features, people or activities are closely recreated, to dramatic expressions of the feelings derived from spending time outside, from composers recreating the sounds of nature to choreographers developing dances that reflect the seasons, the arts can build upon the way we see, feel and interact with the world around us.

Taking the arts outside gives pupils more freedom. Freedom to move, to make more noise, to use a wider range of materials and to be experimental. As a teacher it may take you time to build your confidence to allow that freedom but the results can be creative and inspiring, bringing new elements to pupils' work and helping them to think and work in different ways.

Sketching out the seasons

Subject: Art and design

Key focus: Developing drawing and painting skills by creating a sketchbook

Also
- learning about and using different materials
- developing observational skills

Level: High

Previous learning required:

Mark-making, observational drawing, use of a range of materials such as pencil, charcoal, crayon, marker pens, drawing pens, ink and paint.

Aim of the activity:

To develop observational, drawing and painting skills over the course of a year through the creation of a sketchbook recording seasonal change.

Equipment:

- a sketchbook for each pupil – this could be a bought sketchbook or made at the start of the year by your pupils as an introductory activity.
- access to materials for drawing and painting such as:
  - Pencils
  - Rubbers
  - Charcoal
  - Pastels
  - Crayons
  - Paint
  - Brushes.

Description of the activity:

Sketchbooks have a range of uses: they can be a place to experiment, to develop your skills, to capture ideas and images, for observation and imagination, and a place to start sketches for a new piece of work.

Following the seasons is a great theme for a sketchbook as it provides opportunities to focus in on something specific and stretch out to big ideas. It gives your pupils a chance to make their own decisions within a structure that is easy to understand and flexible enough to make their own.

Let each pupil decide on one subject for the year – it might be a tree or shrub, a view across the playground or the surrounding area or the sky.

Whilst you don't want a sketchbook that feels like a complete mess without any structure, you do want your pupils to be able to experiment and try out new ideas. Some pupils will like drawing accurately, others will like the more experimental activities, so try and provide a mixture over the year. Here are some starting points you might like to use:

- choose your subject and draw it in pencil or charcoal – try again with your wrong hand;
- try to match colours you see at different times of year – note any mixing of colours as reference for future works;
- draw or paint your subject using materials found only in the grounds, such as sticks, leaves and earth;
- make marks in your sketchbook that describe something about your subject that isn't a picture of it – this might be a texture, a shape, or even a representation of a sound it makes.

Progression and extensions:

As the year goes by, let your pupils set their own 'briefs' for their sketchbooks. They might repeat something they did earlier or try something entirely new.

At the end of the year pupils can make a piece of work based on their sketchbook, drawing on ideas and techniques from their year's work. This could be a painting, a sculpture or even a cartoon strip; it could be a collaborative piece used to mark the end of the school year.

Adaptations:

Pupils could develop an electronic sketchbook instead of a paper one. This would require access to suitable programmes and tools, appropriate to pupils' abilities and needs.

Outdoor artist inspiration

Subject: Art and design

THREE PROGRESSIVE ACTIVITIES

Key focus: Learning about artists who work outdoors

Also
- learning about and using different materials

Level: Low, medium and high

Previous learning required:

This series of activities shows progression which could be worked on through the years or across a series of lessons with older pupils. Pupils start with easy-to-understand art and simple techniques and move on to more complex methods and ideas as they progress through their lessons. All activities have a common theme of studying artists who connect their work to their local landscape. Ideally each stage builds on the previous work but they could be undertaken independently of each other.

Aim of the activity:

To learn about artists who create their art outdoors and to use this as inspiration and starting points for pupils' own compositions.

Equipment:

- a search online for each artist's name using the word 'artist' to find images of their work;
- for specific equipment see each level.

Lower-level activity:

Equipment:

- images of Andy Goldsworthy and Kathy Klein's work (both are artists who create ephemeral natural art – choose works that are made from leaves and flowers and form simple patterns, shapes and lines).
- lots of flowers and leaves collected from your grounds and supplemented if necessary with additional flowers or leaves brought into school to ensure you have enough for everyone to work with.

Description of the activity:

Start by looking at the work of Andy Goldsworthy or Kathy Klein. Look specifically at their works using leaves and flowers. Use some of the following questions to discuss their works with your pupils.

- Is there anything particular you like about this work?
- How does it make you feel – happy or sad, peaceful or energetic, wanting to try for yourself or happy to just look?
- How does the colour make you feel?
- What techniques and materials do you think the artist used to create their work?

This activity is best done when there is a good range of colour in the grounds – such as summer for flowers or autumn for leaves.

Go out into the grounds and collect leaves, petals, etc. Make sure that these can be picked and you are not destroying a beautiful display or a wildflower meadow in mid-flower (unless they have been grown to be used in this way). You can always supplement this with additional flowers or leaves brought into school.

Find a space outside, sheltered from the wind so that the work doesn't blow away. Pupils use the leaves and flowers to make their own patterns. Start with everyone creating circles with patterns within them or making curved lines that lead somewhere. Try combining these forms together, with some of the class creating circles and some creating lines that run between and around them.

Take a video of the works you have made – walking alongside the lines and around the circles. Take still photos from different angles and together decide how you can display these in the classroom.

Progressions and extensions:

Instead of using just circles and curved lines weaving between them, ask pupils to find an object in their grounds that they can use as a focal point for their work. They could work together in groups to create something that circles a tree or leads away from a fence or post.

Adaptations:

Use similar materials, maybe with smaller leaves or flowers, for works based in trays or on table-tops, or go large and collect items from the grounds and lay them out inside in the school hall or your classroom.

Middle-level activity:

Equipment:

Raelene Stevens is an aboriginal artist who uses simple patterns, including bright dots and lines, to create her bright images, reflecting the landscape she lives in. You will need images of her art as well as:

- something to 'collect' your colours in – this might be containers, or paper with pens or paint, or colourful magazines that you can tear up for colour matching;
- paints or crayons of different colours, large sheets of paper to work on, something to hold the paper down;
- paint brushes, cotton buds, pieces of sponge to make marks with;
- water to wash hands and brushes, etc., with.

Look back at the work you created based on Andy Goldsworthy or Kathy Klein's work. There you created patterns using leaves and flowers found in the school grounds. This time you are going to create patterns that represent flowers, bricks or other features found in your grounds.

Then look at Raelene Stevens' art. She tries to show what it feels like in her part of the world, the Australian countryside, not by an exact representation but by using colours and shapes that give us an idea of what it is like where she lives. Choose some of the questions and add your own to help pupils explore their feelings about her work. Below are some questions you could use:

- Is there anything particular you like about this work?
- How does it make you feel – happy or sad, peaceful or energetic, wanting to try for yourself or happy to just look?
- Does it matter if it is not a direct representation of the subject? Or is it OK just to be a pattern, colour or series of shapes to help you to feel what it is like?
- What do you think the artist is trying to say in this image?
- Can you tell something about the subject even if it isn't exactly like it is in real life?
- Can you tell if the country is hot or cold from the colours used in the work?
- How does the colour make you feel?
- What techniques and materials do you think the artist used to create their work?

Once you have discussed the art, pupils can go outside and discover the range of colours and shapes in their grounds. If you have planters, a flower bed or meadow you may want to focus on that or you can explore the colours in brickwork, paving slabs, moss and lichens – whatever you have in your grounds. Collect colours by colour matching. This might be with paint, crayons, pieces of paper from magazines or by photographing the different objects.

Ask pupils to pick just three features and work out a way to represent each of them. Working in groups, pupils decide on their subjects – will it be flowers like Raelene, will it be bricks in the wall of the school, or maybe the lines of the railings around your grounds?

The next stage is painting the compositions. If the weather is good why not paint outside? If it is not so good, bring the task back indoors.

Using the three different features that they have chosen, the pupils can now create their art. Remember they are not trying to create a picture of their subject but are creating a feeling using the colours and shapes they have found outside. Use lines, dots and splodges of colour made with paint brushes, sponges or even their fingers and hands. They could place them roughly in the right positions on the paper, or just create patterns with the shapes.

Progressions and extensions:

If pupils have spaces to fill on the page, ask them to come up with a simple motif that they could replicate across the page, maybe changing the colour as appropriate. Look at the images at the beginning of this activity: three main features are represented: flowers (in different colours), trees and bricks/walls. In one of the images the spaces between the main images have been filled with a motif of a circle surrounded by dots. Where this would be grass they are green; where it would be sky they are blue. But there are no hard and fast rules – the aim is to express how the area feels more than what it looks like.

Higher-level activity:

Equipment:

Anthony Gormley uses his own body to model his work on. You will need examples of his work and:

- large sheets of card (at least 150cm square) OR lots of cardboard boxes;
- marker pens and scissors.

This time your pupils are going to be inspired by the work of Anthony Gormley – well known for creating *The Angel of the North*.

Before you look at his work, look back on the work pupils did outside previously. Discuss how they first used materials from outside to create patterns and pathways, then used shapes and colours to show the characteristics of your school grounds.

This time you are going to create 'people' to put into different spaces. This activity is based on the work of Anthony Gormley, who is famous for creating sculptures based on his own body.

Working in groups, pupils identify a space in their grounds in which they want to place their person. They should consider why they have chosen that space, what they want to highlight and how putting someone there will do this. What should that person be doing? They will also need to make sure it is not going to get in the way of anyone or anything if they want to leave it outside for a while.

Using a large sheet of card, one person should lie down on the card, forming a shape that shows some type of activity. It might be sitting; it might be leaping for a ball; it might be watching birds. They then draw around that shape and cut it out, keeping it in one piece so that they end up with a large piece of card with a person-shaped hole in it and a piece of card shaped like the person.

If you are using boxes, either unfold them and cut a shape out (maybe sticking more than one box together) or stack them up to create the basic shape of a person, sitting or standing in your space – see how Anthony Gormley uses box shapes to create some of his figures.

Pupils then add that person to their space. They might like to lay them on the ground or prop them up against a wall so that the pattern of the bricks shows through. If they have created two people, ask them to decide how they want to arrange them in their space or whether they should use two spaces instead of one.

Take a tour of the figures and ask pupils to explain their works, why they chose that action for the person and why that space. Encourage other pupils to ask questions about the works.

Progression and extensions:

Add new features to the cardboard shapes – drawing or painting onto the card or filling spaces with found items from around the grounds.

Adaptations:

Instead of using cardboard shapes, pupils could use small world figures and put them into miniature landscapes, creating the spaces for them to stand or sit in by building mini landscapes from natural materials found in your grounds. Or on a sunny day, pupils could create shadows with their bodies, photographing these in different locations.

Sounds around our grounds

Subject area: Music

Key focus: Explore making sounds

Also
- using musical vocabulary
- links with science – how sounds are made
- links with language and literacy – using descriptive language

Level: Low

Previous learning required:

Pupils should be introduced to making musical sounds and listening to the way different instruments sound in pitch, tone and volume.

Aim of the activity:

To discover the different types of sound that can be made from objects and features found in the grounds.

Equipment:

- a selection of beaters – with different heads;
- clipboards with paper and pencils;
- a piece of paper with pairs of words at each end of a line (see below).

Description of the activity:

Working in small groups, pupils investigate the way different materials sound when they strike them with a particular type of beater.

The aim is to describe each sound using a given selection of pairs of words (see Figure 13.1). The words describe the extremes of different types of sounds and pupils should indicate where along a line between each pair of words they think their sound should belong. Some of the words may be unfamiliar to them, especially in relation to musical sounds, so discuss these, with examples, before they head out on their exploration.

Spiky	Smooth
Gentle	Strong
Rich	Thin
Quiet	Loud
High	Low
Bright	Dull
Warm	Cold
Melodious	Tuneless

Figure 13.1

When back inside discuss the different sounds – did different groups use the same objects or features? Did they come up with similar answers? Why might there be differences? Did they use the same beaters to strike them with, for example?

Progression and extensions:

Are there other words they could use to describe the sounds? Listen to a range of instruments and describe these too. Build a word bank of descriptive words that could be used to describe musical sounds.

This could be extended to describe longer extracts of music too.

Adaptations:

If you have limited space or pupils with limited mobility you could locate the class in one space that is easy to access but away from other classes. Collect different objects and bring them to that location to test out the sounds. Alternatively, pupils could go outside to collect some objects then bring them indoors to test them.

Performance makers

Subject area: Performance: music, dance or drama

THREE PROGRESSIVE ACTIVITIES

Key focus: Performing in front of an audience

Level: Low, medium and high

Previous learning required:

This activity shows progression across the years and builds pupils' ability and confidence in performing in front of other people. Before the first activity they should have some experience of playing, reciting or dancing with other people.

Aim of the activity:

To build confidence in performing in front of other people – whether that is music, drama, dance or some other skill.

Equipment:

This will depend on the performances to be given – from musical instruments or juggling equipment, to costumes and simple sets for drama or dance.

Consider the surface of the space, especially if pupils are undertaking physical activities. You may want to bring out gymnastics mats for example.

You may also want to create a backdrop such as decorated sheets hung on a washing line or moveable structures to create a defined space in which to perform.

Description of the activity:

Performing in a group or on your own can be a difficult task for many – especially if they are not confident in the type of performance being undertaken. Building up gradually in different ways can help pupils gain confidence as well as enjoyment of performing in front of an appreciative audience.

Using the outdoors also makes a performance different: it will change the acoustics; lighting may change throughout the performance; the weather may have an impact; where and how the audience is positioned could affect their view; you could even take the performance into more than one space or move it around the site. Being outside also provides a different atmosphere. It can be more informal than performing indoors and there are different settings you can use, and different situations that you can provide, to change the experience.

Consider whether the audience will sit or stand, which way they are facing (not looking into the sun), and how the seats, if they are being used, are laid out (you could even use rugs on the ground).

All these elements can help to make performing easier as pupils become used to being the centre of attention, and can be considered as part of the class preparations.

Lower-level activity:

To build pupils' confidence in performing to others, start with everyone singing, playing, reading, chanting or dancing together. Clapping games from the playground are a fun way to get things going.

Then divide the pupils into groups and maybe begin with a round or performance where the start is staggered but all perform the same actions or words. Everyone in the group will sing or move together but each group will have their own individual part to play. As pupils build skills and confidence, small groups can join together to perform music, drama or dance to the others in their class.

If you have moveable seating outside you can rearrange this in different ways. Often seating outside is circular or horseshoe in shape, meaning that performers feel less separated from those watching and listening. Singing songs or telling stories around a campfire also takes the pressure off the performers and can therefore be a great way to get started.

Medium-level activity:

As pupils build their confidence and experience of performing to each other in their class, encourage them to perform for others as part of an outdoor assembly or performance – this might be to parents and carers, other classes in a year group or a younger group of pupils.

This time there is more of a focus on their performance and they will have a specific subject to present and an audience to perform to.

Engage your pupils in planning what they are going to perform. What is the topic of the assembly or performance? What songs, poems or theme for a dance will fit with the overall message of the performance?

As part of the preparation consider where your performance is to take place. If you have fairly empty school grounds you may just want to bring chairs outside for your audience, if your grounds are more developed you may be able to use other features such as wooden seats or even an amphitheatre if you are very lucky!

What is the backdrop going to be like? Do you have bushes or a wall behind the performers or would it be an idea to string up some sheets on a washing line behind them – maybe with a scene painted on it? Plan this together with the class as you develop what you are going to perform.

Higher-level activity:

It is now time to do some performing through busking – an activity that generally takes place outside or in large public spaces.

If pupils have other skills beyond music, drama or dance, such as juggling, gymnastics or even comedy, encourage these performances too.

As a group, work out where the best locations for busking are in the grounds. More confident performers might like to perform where more people sit. If you ever have lunch outside, this could be the place for them to be. Others might like to busk in less visited places around the grounds.

Pupils could create a trail between the different locations or a map for the audience to know where they can visit, maybe with the times of performances on.

Progression and extensions:

Pupils can write their own compositions to be performed and their own programme notes to hand out to their audience.

Adaptations:

Performances could be recorded in situ and shown later rather than being performed live.

ARTS ACTIVITIES CAN ALSO BE FOUND WITHIN THE FOLLOWING THEMES:

- Pollinators in your school grounds – illustration, drawing skills, creating models;
- Grow, cook, eat, celebrate – designing signage, prints of leaves and stems, creating inks, etc., from crops, make drawing and painting tools, make charcoal;
- Dig for Victory – make veg into characters to promote home growing, create 3D materials to model or paint heaps of fruit and veg to create a huge Dig for Victory sign, create miniature Dig for Victory gardens;
- Seasonal change – mark-making using seasonal materials and backdrops of colour;
- The Vikings have arrived – clothes, textiles and crafts, including jewellery and sculptures, and natural dyes.

14

Technology including cooking

WHY TAKE TECHNOLOGY OUTDOORS?

Firstly let's just take a moment to define 'technology'. Whilst this does include computers and mobile phones, it also includes the simplest piece of equipment that has been designed using scientific knowledge for a specific function. This could be as simple as a wheel or a potato peeler or as complex as a laptop or video camera. If we use a stick in a specific way, is that technology?

Technology is designed to fix a problem or meet a need and many of those needs can be based outside. Some of the activities in this book that include technology are designed with a fun outcome (see the Crazy golf activity); some are more practical, from building bridges to cooking over a campfire. Some have an environmental purpose such as building a bug hotel, whilst some help us to see how tools and equipment have developed over time.

Looking at the information technology available to use outside, we can discover a wide range of apps that can help us deliver different aspects of the curriculum. Rather than list specific apps that will change over time, we have outlined some of the types of apps you might find useful in the 'Other useful resources' section at the end of the book.

Growing and cooking outdoors bring their own learning potential – from understanding the fire triangle to working safely in a dangerous situation, from building your own growing beds or bird scarers to tasting food you have grown and cooked yourself. Working with fire should only be carried out by someone with knowledge and skills, but these can be easily acquired through training and experience, bringing an additional dimension to pupils' learning outdoors.

Crazy golf

Subject area: Design and technology

Key focus: Design and construction of a product

Also
- evaluation of a product design and implementation
- scale drawing
- analysis of data

Level: High

Previous learning required:

Exploring properties of materials.
   Designing and making simple products.

Aim of the activity:

To design and create a temporary crazy golf course for the school grounds.

Equipment:

- cardboard boxes and tubes;
- ropes and string;
- sticky tape and glue;
- tape measures;
- clipboards, paper, pencils and rulers;
- golf balls and putters (tennis balls and hockey sticks would work too).

Description of the activity:

Pupils will be working in groups to create a series of crazy golf holes that together will make a course.

Start by undertaking research into crazy golf courses. If you are able you could even visit one to give it a try!

Select a location for the course and allocate space to each group. Make sure you know the direction the course will run in, so that one hole leads on to the next. In order that people can start at different places in the course at the same time, create a circular course so that the final hole leads straight onto the first.

The design process for this task will mainly be hands-on experimentation once initial sketches have been created. Set limits on how many pieces of the materials they can use for each hole.

With the materials selected, each group designs their hole, tests it out, makes alterations and gets it ready for others to try. Will the balls have to go through tunnels or tubes? Will the hole run over different levels? How will they create the holes for the ball to end up in? How do you prevent the balls from running away from the course? Pupils should also set a 'par' score for their hole – an expected number of shots to complete the hole.

A plan of the route of the course with the par for each hole can be created either as a scale drawing or using computer graphics, to use as instructions for new users of the course.

The course can then be used by the class and, depending on how robust it is, by others in the school.

Each hole should be evaluated by those who use it and the most successful hole identified. Pupils can develop the criteria for judging a 'successful' hole. This might include: quality of design, robustness of the build, aesthetic quality, how much fun it is to play, ease of play (is that a negative or a positive quality?), etc.

Progressions and extensions:

Pupils can make a scale plan and elevation of their completed structure so that a record is made of it and it can be built again in the future.

Adaptations:

Consider the different skills, ideas and roles pupils can bring to the design, construction and playing of the game, so that everyone is engaged in ways that recognise their abilities and needs. This might include different levels of the course height, the size of the balls being used, the method of projection and whether the ball is steered in any other way.

Building a bridge over a puddle

Subject area: Design and technology

Key focus: Problem-solving through design

Also
- understanding how forces effect the design of a structure
- developing a scientific approach to problem-solving, changing one variable at a time (the scientific method)
- assessing which solutions are most effective

Level: High

Previous learning required:

This activity does not require any previous learning as it harnesses the creativity of open-ended loose parts play to solve design problems. You may want to walk to a local bridge to look at what it is made of, how it is made and what supports it.

Aim of the activity:

To develop problem-solving skills and an awareness of the part forces play in structural design.

Equipment:

- a plentiful assortment of 'loose parts' – logs, pipes or tubes, ropes, planks, newspaper, paper cups, string; water to create puddles or a long length of blue fabric to simulate a river;
- small world figures who will cross your bridges;
- tablets to look up inspirational bridge images and document learning.

Description of the activity:

Begin by splitting the class into small groups or pairs. Introduce the problem to solve, which is to 'design a bridge to enable small world characters to get across the puddle/river without getting wet'.

Each group can use any of the loose parts to solve the problem. Explain that when scientists conduct experiments, they will change one thing (a variable) at a time, so they know what made the difference. Encourage pupils to try different ideas and see what works and what doesn't. Give pupils 15–20 minutes to work with the materials and try out ideas. Next, invite pupils to peer assess another group's efforts. Encourage them to ask open-ended questions of each other to prompt discussion:

- What decisions did you make?
- Why did you do that?
- Did anything go wrong? How did you solve this problem?
- What would you change about your design and why?

Take this opportunity to walk around and interact with your pupils and their designs. Next, give pupils 5 more minutes back at their own bridge to make any final changes before reviewing everyone's solutions as a class. In this final review, draw out their thoughts on why some materials work better than others, demonstrating the part friction plays with smooth and rough surfaces and the effect gravity has on unsupported structures. Document the activity on the tablets and use images or videos to revisit their learning indoors.

Progression and extensions:

Extend the challenge by making the river wider or adding other design considerations such as, 'It must take a certain weight' or 'a vehicle must be able to travel across it'.

Adaptations:

You can differentiate this activity according to the needs of your pupils. For some you may want to introduce an element of narrative to engage their imaginations: 'Is there a crocodile in the water that we don't want to disturb?' For younger pupils you could read *The Three Billy Goats Gruff* or Julia Donaldson's *The Troll*, which feature bridges. For others you could stipulate a time limit to focus their efforts.

TECHNOLOGY ACTIVITIES CAN ALSO BE FOUND WITHIN THE FOLLOWING THEMES:

- Pollination – research, design and build a product;
- The Vikings have arrived – what did the Vikings eat for breakfast? Would I feel at home in a Viking house?
- Seasonal change – cooking – using seasonal ingredients, festival food.

PART 3
MORE PRACTICAL ACTIVITIES AND RESOURCES

15
Quick activity ideas and techniques

Quick activities

Subject area: Ranging across different subject areas

Key focus: Ideas to get pupils energised, to fill gaps in lessons, or where some pupils complete work ahead of others

Level: Low, medium and high

Previous learning required:

None.

Aim of the activity:

To create a bank of ideas that can be used with a group to energise them, warm them up, to fill a gap in the lesson or to finish it off. Or for pupils who have completed work ahead of others.

Lower-level activities:

Marching

Equipment:

- no equipment required.

Description of the activity:

Marching around your grounds counting together as you go. Take it in turns to decide if you are going forwards or backwards or if you start at a specific number, i.e. not at 1. As you march around the grounds count the number of steps between two objects or places. When you reach your destination, count the number of steps as you march to the next location.

You can also use rhymes to march to. Start the rhyme below by marching on your left leg to the words 'had' and 'don't', and you should end up marching on your left leg when you chant 'left' and on your right leg when you chant 'right'.

> He had a good home and he left, pause, left, pause, left, pause. Don't you think that he was right, pause, right, pause, right.

Pupils can then make up their own new marching rhymes.

Sequencing events

Equipment:

- for some activities it would be useful to have cards with pictures or descriptions of different events on them.

Description of the activity:

Sequencing events by lining up in order. The order that you choose could be as simple as lining up in alphabetical order or birthdays or you could hand out pictures or words describing different things that happen in the school day, or things that happen in nature throughout the year.

Telling the time

Equipment:

- chalk or string to mark out the clocks with.

Description of the activity:

Pupils, working in small groups, should draw out clocks on the ground. The teacher calls out different times and two pupils from each group lie down on the ground to indicate the time – one has their hands by their side for the hour hand, the other has their hands above them for the minute hand. After the first time, pupils from each group can take it in turns to call out a time and pupils within the groups take it in turns to 'tell the time'.

Measuring using non-standard units

Equipment:

- no equipment required.

Description of the activity:

Measure the length of the playground, football pitch or other large area using the non-standard unit of pupils standing in a line with their arms out horizontally to the side. Before each attempt, pupils can guess how many of them it will take to measure the length.

Medium-level activities:

Descriptive vocabulary

Equipment:

- found items to be collected as part of the activity.

Description of the activity:

Working in pairs, pupils collect two sets of six objects as near to identical as possible. This might be leaves, pebbles, sticks, blades of grass – whatever is available. They have one set each and sit back-to-back. One lays out the objects on the ground and describes what they are doing to their partner, who has to try and replicate what is made. They can describe as they work, or when the picture is completed. This develops vocabulary and also listening skills. As pupils get used to this activity their pictures can become more complex, for example layering items to create 3D structures.

Our school grounds alphabet

Equipment:

- none required – although you can write the alphabet out onto large sheets of paper, spreading the letters out evenly on the sheet and placing the found objects next to the letter. (If the object is not movable this can be written next to the letter instead.)

Description of the activity:

Send pupils on a hunt around your grounds for items that start with the different letters of the alphabet. You can allow pupils to get quite creative with their descriptions of their objects as long as they can justify that they represent a specific letter.

This can be developed so that they spell different words or you can apply rules to the collection of the objects, for example the description has to include an adjective.

Finding art in the grounds

Equipment:

- found objects.

Description of the activity:

Pupils can use found objects from their grounds to make pictures or patterns. This might be related to the topic you are working on, for example a mathematical pattern or the parts of a tree, or just be a creative activity in itself.

Higher-level activities:

Groups of things

Equipment:

- clipboard, paper and pencils.

Description of the activity:

Set a criteria for finding groups of things – these might be things that are taller than 10m, things that have at least two lines of symmetry, things that have double letters in them (e.g. tree, litter), or things that are more than 100 years old, etc.

Pupils 'collect' these items by writing them down and share them with the class.

Making faces

Equipment:

- natural materials found in the ground.

Description of the activity:

Working in groups, collect together found items from around the grounds. Choose one pupil from each group as a subject and ask the others to make a representation of their face with the objects on the ground. The other groups have to try to identify whose face it is.

Kennings

Equipment:

- clipboard, paper and pencils.

Description of the activity:

Pupils create kennings about features or areas of their grounds, or the activities that take place there. Kennings are compound descriptors such as 'warmth giver' to describe a fire or 'squirrel's playground' for a tree.

Techniques

● **Postbox revision**

Equipment:

- a series of boxes (shoebox size is ideal) with 'letter box' holes in the front and 'answers' on the top;
- lots of 'letters' to post – these are the clues to help you find the right boxes to post them into.

Description of the activity:

This activity works particularly well for revision of a topic. You need to take your topic and come up with a series of questions and answers – this can be as simple as matching colours or shapes, or as complex as a variety of sums with the same answers (see the image above).

Write the answer to the questions on the boxes and questions on the cards. You will need at least five boxes and enough cards for everyone in the class to have more than two goes – your pupils will keep going as long as you have cards to give them.

Pupils can work in teams, with each team being given the name of a letter. One person from each team collects a letter at random from the person in charge and their number is written on the back of the card. This is so you can check for the winning team. The pupils with the cards then have to find the right box to post them into, before they return to their team and the second person collects a card, again with their number put onto it before they deliver it into the correct box. In other words, it works like a relay race.

As they progress you will find some really great communication skills develop, as those who have been out searching already direct new runners to the right box.

When you run out of cards, or time, collect in all the boxes. The winning team is the one that posted the most *correct* answers. You can identify the teams from the letters that have been written on the back of each card.

This game can also be used as a fun energiser – maybe matching shapes or colours – and can be used over and over again. As pupils move up the school the clues and answers can get harder and harder!

Trails

Equipment:

- luggage labels with instructions on (or ready for new instructions and pens) or another similar way of displaying the clues.

Description of the activity:

Create clues, instructions or questions in a route around the grounds for pupils to follow. The instructions could be clues to where the next label is to be found or an activity to be undertaken. Alternatively the location of the clues can be marked on a map for pupils to follow, maybe each pupil starting at a different point in the trail.

Pupils can create trails themselves too – setting out the route and clues or activities for others to follow along the way.

Sharing information between groups

Equipment:

- flip chart paper and pens;
- information on the topic if required;
- clothesline and pegs.

Description of the activity:

This is a good activity for older pupils when they are researching a new topic or revising one they have just completed.

Starting in groups with some flip chart paper and pens, one person acts as a scribe. Each group is given a different question about the topic to discuss – if it is a new topic provide some information for them to look at or an activity for them to undertake. If it is a revision exercise they should discuss this within the group. The scribe writes notes addressing the group's question as they discuss it or at the conclusion of the discussion. You will need to set a time for this.

The scribe then remains where they are and the rest of the group moves to where a different scribe is located. The scribe explains what has been written so far and the group then add their own research or thoughts.

Move the groups around a couple of times before sharing all the learning between the class. This can be done as presentations by the groups or everything can be hung up on a line or on a fence for all to read.

Using technology

Equipment:

- this will be specific to each activity you undertake.

Description of the activity:

Technology includes the clipboard you take outside, the watch on your wrist to keep time and the tablet pupils record images and data on during lessons outside.

It also includes the range of apps that are available to you to enhance your outdoor learning, from those that help you identify plants and animals to those that record or analyse data. More information on these can be found in Chapter 17.

Don't be afraid to take technology outside – but make sure you are using this as a tool to help you teach so that it does not become the focus of the activity itself, but rather a way of engaging your pupils with the world around them.

Filming outside

Equipment:

- one or more still or video cameras, depending on the activity.

Description of the activity:

Filming activity outside can be a great way to engage pupils in a topic; it can also be useful for revision or for you to record the activity that has taken place. You can use video or stills depending on the resources you have and whether your pupils have the skills needed to get a reasonable recording of what is going on.

If using video you can make your pupils into reporters or presenters, telling the story of the activity they have been working on. Explaining learning to someone else is a great way to ensure it has really been understood and will help to embed it. In a similar way pupils can story-board their work – either as a preparation to an activity or as an explanation incorporating photographs of what they have been doing.

Photography can also be used in the arts to capture performances or processes, rehearsals or ephemeral art.

For you as a teacher, using video and photography can be useful to capture what has been going on in class. This can help you assess the work or use the images to remind pupils of what they did outside. Sometimes, when reviewing the images, you will spot things you didn't notice at the time and this can also be useful in your assessment of the activity.

Using loose parts

Equipment:

- a range of loose parts from natural materials to sports or play equipment depending on the activity.

Description of the activity:

As well as supporting different learning styles, pupil communication and negotiation skills are enhanced, providing pupils with opportunities to risk assess, persevere and develop responsibility for themselves and others.

The benefits of play for children are well known and evidenced, and include improved physical activity, dexterity and supporting intellectual curiosity. Play too is part of the learning process. Schools that develop their outdoor play provision commonly report:

- improvements in behaviour;
- classes that settle more quickly after break time;
- children who are happier and more content in school;
- self-led learning that happens during playtime without active teacher input.

As well as providing a wealth of play experiences and self-led learning opportunities, access to loose materials in school grounds can help bring the curriculum to life through practical, hands on experiences.

Access to loose materials during class time helps build on these skills and experiences, providing an interactive and practical way to teach aspects of the curriculum using materials pupils are familiar with. Below are just a few ways you can incorporate loose parts into your teaching practice.

- Finding and collecting natural materials in the grounds can support pupils' experience of seasonal change and the development of a natural alphabet.
- Small world resources are beneficial in bringing stories to life and for supporting an introduction to scale.
- Make use of a tarpaulin or parachute for numeracy games, for example swap places under the parachute if you are an odd number or a multiple of two.
- Explore angles and shapes using sticks and incorporate a range of materials to explore symmetry.
- Support listening, talking and writing through role play and, using pupil reflection, capture the learning through functional writing, for example writing instructions for a game or persuasive writing based on outdoor experience.
- STEM can be incorporated into lessons, for example challenge your pupils to create an obstacle course to help learn prepositions. Estimate, build and measure a tower. Build a waterproof den and then become an estate agent and market your creation.
- Construct ball runs to explore angles, speed, distance, time and friction.

Outdoor museums and art galleries

Equipment:

- a space and method for displaying your artefacts;
- the artefacts themselves;
- labels or other ways of providing information about the artefacts.

Description of the activity:

Why not create outdoor displays on a theme? You might like to create some of the items for display or invite pupils (and staff) to bring in some items from home. Remember you will be displaying them outside so they will either need to be OK left outdoors or be able to be taken down if necessary. Work with pupils to consider how best to display your items. Will they be labelled? Is there an order to view them in? Is there part of the grounds that would be best to display them in or should they take you on a trail around the grounds? Should some parts be inside and some outside?

Themes might include:

- objects made from wood;
- gardening tools;
- interesting found objects (this could be a miniature display);
- things that look like other things (e.g. pieces of wood, stones or shells);
- items that reflect the cultural heritage of the local community.

Bringing in experts

Equipment:

- experts!
- any additional space or equipment will depend on who you bring into the school grounds.

Description of the activity:

Pupils will always be more interested in an expert coming into the school than learning something from their everyday teacher! Consider who an expert might be and how they can add to your pupils' learning experience. In the science activities we talk about bringing in wildlife experts. Here are some other 'experts' who could help make your times outside even more engaging:

- Parents and grandparents who went to the school themselves – they could talk about how the grounds have changed, if they had lessons outside and what their favourite playground games were.
- Local artists who work outside, especially those who live and work in your local area. Depending on their skills they may be able to lead an art activity with pupils or work with them to create a new feature for your grounds.
- Street performers and buskers can bring energy and entertainment to your grounds. They could both perform their acts and teach pupils new skills. This might even lead to a regular lunchtime performance slot in your grounds.
- Pigeon fanciers. This is a great way to engage pupils with maps. If you release pigeons in your grounds what route will they use to get home? Estimate the time they will arrive home. Will they be faster or slower than if you went by car or train?
- Local faith groups and community members. Can they tell you stories of your local area, of the community that lives there, their traditions and beliefs? Do they have festivals and feasts that you could learn about and take part in? Are there different foods that your pupils might not have tasted before? Could any of these be cooked outside?

Presenting pupils' work

Equipment:

- ways to display work outside – whether under cover or in the open.

Description of the activity:

Every school wall indoors has pupils' work displayed for all to see. This is a celebration of what you do in school and shows pupils how you value their work. If you are going to be working outside more, perhaps you can display some of their work outside too.

You will need to consider how being outside might affect the work. Is it waterproof? Can you give it some protection from the weather? How long will you display it outside? Are there locations that would be particularly good to display things – fences, shelters, walls? Can some of the work become permanent features?

Revisiting

Equipment:

- the equipment will be different for each activity.

Description of the activity:

The school year and the changing seasons provide you with an opportunity to revisit topics and themes. This helps to reinforce what you have done before and gives you opportunities to build, progress and embed the learning. Remember, your pupils will only have seen between six and eleven springs in their lifetime, so there is a lot for them to see and learn about each year.

Things change from year to year too: sometimes spring will be sunny and warm, sometimes wet and windy. This can help you keep the curriculum fresh whilst giving some structure to how you work outside.

16
Themes

TEACHING THROUGH THEMES OUTDOORS

Most of the activities in this book are designed around a specific topic within a curriculum area, but in this section we have taken a group of themes that work well outside and identified a range of activities within each theme, each with links to a curriculum area.

These themes have been written to inspire you to think about how you can plan your curriculum and to show you how cross-curricula teaching can be built around an outdoor theme rather than give you every bit of detail of each activity you might do. In some schools a class may work on a theme on its own, in other schools a whole year group may focus on a theme together, whilst in some schools a theme might be used for the whole school or a whole week of themed activities. We have, therefore, not indicated levels for these activities – we want you to have the flexibility to adapt these to your own needs, seeing what is possible and tweaking our ideas to fit with your pupils' knowledge, abilities and experiences.

You can also take individual activity ideas out of a theme and teach it as a lesson activity in its own right, or move it into a theme of your own.

As you move forward in your outdoor teaching we hope you will look at your schemes of work in a similar way to these themes and identify activities, lessons or progressions of work you can take into your school grounds.

Our first two themes are built around a growing area and show how having a resource like this can lead onto different themes for your cross curriculum work. We have also shown how you can develop themes in different ways, using the seasonal year or taking history as a theme and linking it with other subjects. We hope this will help you see how themes can be flexible or structured and fit in with whatever approach your school uses.

Grow, cook, eat, celebrate!

Subject areas:

- Science
    - living things
    - the seasons
    - what plants need to live
    - changes of state through cooking
    - temperature change
- Maths and numeracy
    - measuring growing areas
    - money and costing

- comparing air miles
- measuring the success of the harvest

• Language and literacy

- retrieving information from different sources
- writing from personal experience
- camp fire stories

• Cookery

- a range of savoury and sweet recipes

• Art and design

- designing signage
- prints from leaves and stems
- creating inks from crops
- making drawing and painting tools including charcoal

• Religious and moral education

- links with faith groups and festivals

Key focus: The cross-curricula potential of growing food in school

Level: Suitable across different levels, choose and adapt to fit your needs

Previous learning required:

None is essential but some previous growing, cooking and time around a fire (if that activity is chosen) would be beneficial.

Aim of the activity:

To use the theme of growing and cooking food as a way to apply learning across a range of subject areas including:

- science
- maths and numeracy
- language and literacy
- cookery
- art and design
- religious and moral education.

Equipment (across all activities):

- a growing area – from a small pot of herbs to a polytunnel and raised beds;
- gardening equipment as required for the crops you grow;
- a campfire, fire pit or camp stove for any cooking activity;
- water to wash crops, equipment and yourselves with;
- clipboards, paper and pencils;
- see also each curriculum area for additional specific equipment needed.

Description of the activity:

Within this theme we are looking at ways that food growing and cooking can help to support a range of areas across the curriculum, and you may find others too. We have given general descriptions and ideas for you to adapt and make your own according to the age and ability of your class. We hope this sparks some creative learning opportunities for your pupils.

Science

Equipment required in addition to that listed above:

- water;
- compost;
- plants that can be monitored as they grow (or don't!);
- food to cook and equipment to cook with;
- a temperature gun.

Description of the activity:

Tap into a range of topics within the science curriculum – and not just biology. Below are a few suggestions to help you get started.

- Living things – recognising things that are living, non-living and things that have lived in your growing area.
- The seasons – observing the change in your growing area across the seasons. Why do we plant things at different times of year?
- The requirements for plants to live – investigate the different requirements for plants to grow: water, food, light, soil, air. Test out some of your crops to see what happens when you remove one of these factors – extend this by experimenting with different crops.
- Cooking – investigate how different crops change when heated/cooked and when different ingredients are combined together.
- Investigate temperature changes as you light your fire and cook your food – plot this on graphs.

Maths and numeracy

Equipment required in addition to that listed above:

- tape measures;
- scales.

Description of the activity:

Maths is vital in the planning, harvesting and cooking of your crops. Here are just a few ways you can bring maths into your growing area:

- Measure out your growing area. If you have existing beds measure these, calculate the perimeter, area and volume of your growing beds. If you want new beds, do the same calculations as you plan what and where you want to add to your site.
- How much will it cost you to grow different crops? How does this compare with the cost of them in the shops? Why might that be?
- How far do the crops you grow travel in comparison with the crops in the shops? Calculate the different air miles for different crops.
- Estimate and measure the success of your harvest. You could measure your sweet corn or runner bean stems from week to week and plot a graph of the change, maybe even comparing this to the weather.
- How much have we produced? Use estimation and measurements to discover the volume and weight of different crops.
- Measure and plot out your harvest success over the months. Which is the most productive month for individual crops or perhaps the whole growing area? Which is the best measure of success – weight, number of items harvested or value of the crop?

Language and literacy

Equipment required in addition to that listed above:

- gardening and cookery books or websites and seed packets.

Description of the activity:

Your growing and cooking areas will contain a wonderful assortment of sights, smells and tastes. This provides many opportunities for the use and development of language.

- Retrieve information from different sources to learn how to grow and cook your crops. Research a range of crops and how to grow them from the internet, gardening books and seed packets.

- Write from personal experience, describing the processes you have undertaken in the growing and cooking of your own food.
- Campfires are always great places to tell stories and get conversations going. The format of sitting around a fire can make it easier for some to open up and become part of the discussions, especially if they are talking about their favourite campfire food!

Cookery

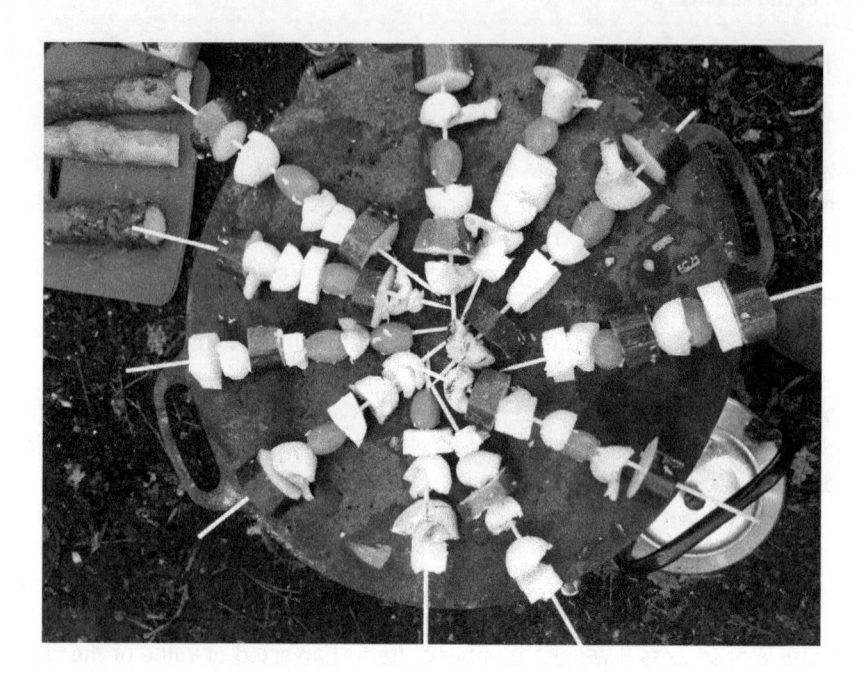

Equipment required in addition to that listed above:

- cooking equipment, depending on what you want to cook, such as long handled tongs and oven gloves or similar;
- implements for eating with;
- equipment to wash with;
- a first-aid kit that includes something for dressing burns.

Description of the activity:

Campfire cooking, whether over a real fire or camp stove, is an activity your pupils will love. Somehow, cooking outdoors is always exciting, maybe because we seem closer to the cooking going on. But how often do you take your cookery lessons outdoors?

If you do not have the experience and confidence to cook food outside consider simple food preparation such as salads – both of vegetables and fruit – to get you started. Cooking around a fire is great fun but you will need to take turns in who can access the fire to ensure safety.

This is an area of teaching outside where you will have to consider health and safety more than many other lesson activities outdoors. You will need to make sure anyone leading this activity is safe working with children around a fire or camp stove and you will need to make sure you are as careful outside with hygiene as you are indoors.

Fire-lighting can be a safe activity if you prepare and structure the activity well. The food does not have to be complex and if your pupils have grown the fruit and vegetables themselves they will be even more enthusiastic – and may well try eating food they have never tried before!

- Why not start with creating salads outside – both with vegetables and fruit?
- Marshmallows and S'mores (toasted marshmallows squashed between biscuits and chocolate) are always popular! (Make sure you have a suitable supply for your pupils as many are made with gelatine.)
- Vegetable and fruit kebabs work well. Use wooden or bamboo skewers soaked in water before use.
- Vegetables with herbs and oil or fruit with cinnamon in foil packages work well on a fire. But do make sure they don't burn by placing them on areas of the fire that have died down a little and turning them regularly.
- As you gain confidence in cooking outside, build up a range of recipes, including soups and stews.

You can develop this activity as you try out food from around the world, cooked using different methods over the campfire. Consider inviting in family, friends and members of the local community who have expertise and knowledge of food from a range of cultures.

Art and design

Equipment required in addition to that listed above:

- a range of art equipment such as pencils, crayons and paints.

Description of the activity:

The seasonal change of plants in your growing area, gardening tools and even activities outside are great subjects for representational art. However, also think about other ways you can get creative in your growing and cooking area:

- How about designing signage for your crops? This might be images of the fruit and vegetables on pebbles, elaborate signs or seed packet covers.
- Why not make prints from leaves and stems?

- Explore creating inks, dyes or other pigments from the crops you produce.
- Make drawing and painting tools out of sticks and leaves.
- Make charcoal (or collect any created by your fire) and use this for drawing what you have seen around the fire.

Religious and moral education

Equipment required in addition to that listed above:

- specific foods that are mentioned in sacred texts or may be required for festivals.

Description of the activity:

There are many religious festivals where food features strongly, whether blessing crops as they grow or when harvested, to different foods and meals eaten as part of festival celebrations.

- Make links with local faith groups to find out how you can work together to mark festivals in your school grounds that include food in the celebrations or commemorations.
- Plan your crops for the following year to include fruit and vegetables that have links to different faiths. This might include food mentioned within religious texts which can then be used to help make those stories come alive. Or they could be crops mentioned in parables or food eaten by people within sacred texts.

Progression and extensions:

Why not end this theme with a celebration with food at its heart? Pupils can be divided into groups to be given responsibility for planning different elements. This might include:

- notification and invitations to the event;
- decorating the area where everything is taking place;
- planning a timetable for the event including getting everything ready;
- devising recipes and cooking;
- serving the guests;
- recording the event – photographs and journalistic writing for the school newsletter or website.

You can also make links to the Dig for Victory theme.

More possible curriculum links:

- History – make links with Dig for Victory or food eaten at different times in history.
- Design and technology – design and create features for your growing area such as raised beds, irrigation systems and scarecrows.

- Geography – investigate the origin of different crops. Visit the local supermarket to find out the range of crops there and how far they have travelled. Compare the air miles to those grown in your school grounds.
- Maths – set up a farmers' market. How much have your crops cost to produce? How much do we sell them for? Can you add value by turning your crops into something more profitable, for example jam or chutney?

Adaptations:

Growing can be on any scale – from herbs in pots to polytunnels and raised beds. Make sure that planting is accessible by considering not only the height of pots and beds but also the reach across a bed and the materials used on pathways between your features. Check the width of paths and the doorway into a greenhouse or polytunnel.

Dig for Victory

Subject areas:

- History
    - exploring the origin of Dig for Victory gardens
    - researching how Dig for Victory gardens were made
    - tools over the years
    - writing and performing speeches to support the war-effort
- Design and technology
    - designing your growing area
    - how to organise plants
- Science
    - comparing growing heritage seeds with modern varieties
    - learning about the parts of a plant

- Cooking and nutrition
    - using simple cookery equipment as in the 1940s
    - taste testing edible flowers and food saving recipes
    - re-growing vegetables
- MFL
    - learning the names of different plants in other languages
    - reporting back to another home country about Dig for Victory
- Literacy
    - writing Dig for Victory garden diaries
    - make radio jingles and adverts for your crops
    - train another group in how to make a Dig for Victory garden
    - write technical advice on growing crops
- Art and design
    - make vegetable characters
    - make pictures from fruit and vegetables
    - create miniature gardens

Key focus: The cross-curricula project on the historical theme of Dig for Victory

Level: Suitable across different levels, choose and adapt to fit your needs

Previous learning required:

Some understanding of what the Dig for Victory campaign was, in the context of the Second World War.

Aim of the activity:

To use a historical theme as a means for exploring what it was like to grow your own food during wartime and to develop skills across a range of other curriculum areas including:

- design and technology;
- science;
- cooking and nutrition;
- modern foreign languages;
- literacy;
- art.

Equipment (across all curriculum areas):

- an outdoor area for growing, which might include raised beds or containers;
- an outdoor water supply;
- an outdoor space for activities including discussions and drawing;
- clipboards, paper, pencils.

Description of the activity:

Within this theme we are exploring the making and use of productive gardens, using limited resources, to support a range of curriculum areas and skills. We have given general descriptions and ideas for you to adapt and make your own according to the age and ability of your class.

History

Equipment required in addition to that listed above:

- string;
- canes;
- tape measure;
- sign-making materials such as wooden boards, paint and brushes;
- photos of gardens people made during the war.

Description of the activity:

Discuss why people had Dig for Victory gardens and explain that during the war people were encouraged to grow their own produce so that everyone had access to enough good food, and this helped to fill some of the gaps that were left by rationing.

Through this activity your pupils will experience how people planned their vegetable plots and what equipment they needed – then they will start planning their own!

- Explore and find areas in the school grounds that could be used for a vegetable plot or container garden. Modelling your garden on one of the old photos, measure out the space you want to use and mark it out with string and canes. You could take photographs of the process and age them, so they look like wartime pictures.
- If you already have a growing area in your grounds, consider features you could add to make it more like a Dig for Victory garden.
- Consider the tools and equipment needed to make and maintain a garden and how to use and store them. Have tools used in gardens changed much since the war?
- Create signs or an interpretation board to help others understand the Dig for Victory garden.
- Write and perform speeches to promote the benefits of digging for victory, for ordinary people and the overall war-effort.

Design and technology

Equipment required in addition to that listed above:

- used wooden planks or logs, or recycled items such as car tyres, containers or plastic sacks;
- potting compost or topsoil;
- found sticks;
- permanent marker pens.

Description of the activity:

Making somewhere to grow vegetables and fruit can be a creative design challenge, especially when using recycled materials, like people had to during the war.

- Design and make your vegetable growing area: for a vegetable bed use old wooden planks or logs as borders; if you are creating a container garden, keep costs down and be more authentic by re-purposing containers, but do make sure that whatever you use hasn't been contaminated by any toxic chemicals that could leach into your crop. They can be decorated using left-over paint.
- Decide how you will organise the plants and use sticks and a marker pen to design large labels ready for marking where your crops will be sown or planted – they can be written or pictorial.

Science

Equipment required in addition to that listed above:

- seeds, plants, tubers or cuttings for growing vegetables and fruit;
- garden tools such as spades, forks, trowels, watering can;
- minibeast identification sheets.

Description of the activity:

Sowing, growing and nurturing vegetables and fruit have multiple science links and opportunities for life skills and wellbeing that are useful in peace time as well as in difficult times like war.

- Potatoes and runner beans are classic wartime vegetables that grow easily in containers or vegetable plots. Search online for 'Heritage seeds' to find different varieties and compare the results with modern seeds.
- Learn about different parts of plants and how they produce new plants, for example runner beans (beans are seeds), potatoes (tubers have eyes) and strawberries (produce runners).

- Why not draw the root structures of the plants you are growing on the side of your containers as if you can see underground?
- Investigate and identify which minibeasts are attacking your crops. Research and try out sustainable ways to deter pests and protect plants that might have been used in wartime: sharp grit or copper tape for deterring slugs and snails and twiggy sticks between plants to put cats off.

Cooking

Equipment required in addition to that listed above:

- some vegetables that could have been grown in Britain;
- camp stove and lighter;
- utensils for preparing, cooking and eating;
- water;
- simple wartime recipes;
- any additional ingredients;
- used plastic cartons;
- a first-aid kit that includes something for dressing burns.

Description of the activity:

As well as a smaller range of foodstuffs during wartime, many people at the time lived in homes with limited cooking facilities. A similar experience can be re-created by cooking on a camp stove outdoors. Wasting food was frowned upon and activities that are about different ways of throwing less food away are just as relevant today.

- Creating a meal on a camp stove using a limited range of ingredients could be a class collaboration or a team challenge.
- Setting up a taste and no waste challenge which includes some food and edible flowers that you have grown. Nasturtiums, calendula and rocket flowers are all edible, as are the shoots on pea plants and the fresh top growth of broad bean plants.
- Have a go at re-growing vegetables. Potatoes, lettuce, onions, celery and others can be re-grown from their root ends or stumps.

Art

Equipment required in addition to that listed above:

- modelling materials like play dough or clay;
- painting materials;
- examples of Archimboldo's fruit and vegetable paintings;
- wire and small sticks for modelling.

Description of the activity:

- Spend time getting to know and coming up with interesting descriptions for home-grown foods, including some challenges such as asking what does that potato or onion look like or remind you of. Then make your chosen vegetable into a character with a message for a postcard promotion about growing and eating it.
- Using Archimboldo's art as a starting point, use 3D modelling materials or painting or drawing to create a heap of vegetables, fruits, seeds and leaves with which to make a huge class Dig for Victory sign or a message about growing and eating fruit and vegetables.
- Create miniature, model Dig for Victory gardens on tiny plots outdoors. Pupils could create figures and tools too and take photographs.

Modern foreign languages

Equipment required in addition to that listed above:

- writing and sketching materials;
- cameras or tablets;
- wood cookies (thin slices of wood);
- marker pens.

Description of the activity:

Learning the English and foreign language names for different things in the garden can be fun and provide skills for life. You could do these activities based around a vegetable garden or by arranging some vegetables and tools in the school grounds and imagining the harvesting has just taken place.

- Guessing which names go with which vegetables – can pupils work out both the English and foreign language names? You could use wood cookies with sounds on to do this as a phonics activity.
- Pupils could pretend to be wartime allies or spies, reporting back to their country about Britain's Dig for Victory campaign. Make a sketch, plan or photograph of the garden and label the vegetables, fruit and tools in a different language, or create different language labels for the plants that are growing.
- If there are fruits and flowers that can be tasted in the garden, pupils could learn how to say which ones they like, what the flavours remind them of and to describe their colours and shapes.

Literacy

Equipment required in addition to that listed above:

- writing materials or electronic devices.

Description of the activity:

Dig for Victory was a campaign that combined striking images with slogans and promotional messaging. Basic UK-grown foods still need promoting for healthy lifestyles today, so pupils could develop their persuasive speaking and writing skills and use images and text to create materials which encourage growing and eating ordinary, healthy food.

- Pupils who have had a hand in growing vegetables could write a weekly diary reporting how the growing is progressing.
- Incorporating music, pupils could create radio jingles, TV advertisements or promotional songs for the campaign.
- Handing more responsibility over to the class, pupils could design an outdoor training activity for another class about Dig for Victory and how we can benefit by doing the same today. Making some teaching materials could be part of the process.
- Writing for a scientific or technical audience, describing the features and uses of garden tools and equipment and advising on how to use them safely.

Progression and extensions:

Pupils could create container gardens related to other history themes:

- medicinal herb gardens or containers;
- Native American gardens with squashes, beans and sweetcorn.

More possible curriculum links:

- Maths – rationing activities using garden produce; weighing the potatoes to find the heaviest of the crop; estimating weights of produce; pricing and selling produce; working out the cost of growing the produce.
- Citizenship – selling produce to raise money for a charity; showing other schools how to start a garden.

Adaptations:

Produce can be grown in many kinds of containers if watered well, for example old plastic sacks propped upright with drainage holes cut into the base, window boxes, wall-mounted containers and hanging baskets.

If gardening or container growing at school is not an option, you could take pupils to visit a vegetable or community garden or allotment and they could take photos or videos. Many of the activities could be done later using bought produce, and using their photos and memories of their visit.

Seasonal change

Subject areas:

- Science
    - life cycles and reproduction – plants and animals and interdependence
    - the movement of the moon

- Religious and moral education
    - rights of passage
    - festivals and events throughout the year

- Language and literacy
    - diaries and journals
    - looking from here ...
    - the sporting year

- Art and design
    - see sketching the seasons
    - using seasonal materials – ice and snow, flowers and seeds, sun and rain
- Geography
    - climate and weather
    - how things change
- Cooking
    - using seasonal ingredients
    - festival food

Key focus: The cross-curricula potential of working with the seasons

Level: All – find the activities that work best for your class and adapt it to make it your own, or work across the school on the theme and share out the activities across the years and classes.

Previous learning required:

An understanding of how the seasons change over a year and that this is repeated every year.
Being introduced to the idea that, whilst the same seasons repeat each year, the timing of these and what they are like can change. Some of this is down to climate change.

Aim of the activity:

To use the theme of change through the seasons to link activities together over a range of subjects throughout the school year, giving opportunities to return and review topics, reinforcing learning and emphasising different areas of the theme.

- Science
    - life cycles and reproduction
    - plants and animals
    - interdependence
    - the movement of the moon
- Religious and moral education
    - rights of passage
    - festivals and events throughout the year
- Language and literacy
    - keeping diaries and journals
    - descriptive writing
    - non-fictional writing

- Art and design
    - see sketching the seasons activity
    - using seasonal materials
- Geography
    - climate and weather
    - how things change
- Cookery
    - using seasonal ingredients
    - festival food

Equipment (across all curriculum areas):

- clipboards, paper and pencils;
- your school grounds or local 'walk to' space that you can access throughout the year and that shows some change – be that the weather or something growing (just one tree is enough);
- see also each curriculum area for additional specific equipment needed.

Science

Equipment required in addition to that listed above:

- access to plants that you can observe every year to see how they change over the seasons – and from year to year;
- you may want to use the 'Science activity – your school grounds food chains';
- information about the phases of the moon – see a 'moon phases' website.

Description of the activity:

Below are a few suggestions linked to the theme of 'Seasonal change':

- Investigate how the plants and animals living in your school grounds are affected by the seasons. This might be as simple as observing deciduous trees and shrubs or perennial plants such as daffodils or snowdrops, observing them at the same time year after year. Each year plants will flower at a slightly different time – plot out the weather (temperature, rain fall) against flowering times to see how these change from one year to the next.
- Identify which animals depend on the plants you grow and investigate the impact this might have on their life cycles. Climate change will impact on the timing of seasons and therefore could make a difference to the animals that live in your grounds in the future.

- Often we talk about the moon coming out at night, but in reality it can often be observed in the daytime too. It is obviously safer to observe the moon than the sun, so it is a good subject to study in the sky. Notice how it waxes and wanes over a month (waxing is the period from the new moon to the full moon, waning is the period after the full moon to the next new moon). A moon phases website will give you the phases of the moon and the time and place it is visible in the sky. You will need to check this as it will not always be visible during the school day, but you could just pop outside when you see it in the sky.

Religious and moral education

Equipment required in addition to that listed above:

- access to information about different rights of passage across different faiths and cultures (both historically and today) such as baptism and other naming ceremonies, and coming of age ceremonies including bar mitzvah and bat mitzvah;
- information about faith festivals that take place throughout the year and that can be celebrated outdoors, for example the festivals of Sukkot, Holi or Harvest.

Description of the activity:

Reflecting on how different faiths and cultures mark the stages in children's lives as they grow up, consider making your own 'rights of passage' activities that take place every year.

Over history many societies and faiths have marked points in the life of young people, such as becoming an adult. Investigate these across a range of faiths and ask pupils to share their own experiences of ceremonies or occasions they have been part of.

You may then like to set up your own 'rights of passage' that become regular and important features of each year in your school – activities that only happen with a particular year group and become something special for pupils of that age. They can grow into features of your school's culture and traditions.

Here are a few suggestions of the type of activities you could consider:

- creating a sculpture in the grounds as a year group;
- every child in a year group plants a bulb in the school grounds – perhaps ready to be picked later in the year;
- outdoor cooking of a unique recipe only carried out by a particular year group at a special time of year;
- one year group creates an outdoor game that everyone else then plays during one particular week;
- a camping weekend in the school grounds by one year group.

Many faiths use the outdoors for festivals and events throughout the year. Try to find at least one event a term that pupils can engage with outside.

Language and literacy

Equipment required in addition to that listed above:

- blank diaries or journals;
- cameras (optional);
- information about the school's sporting activity throughout the year.

Description of the activity:

Throughout the school year there will be different things that take place in your school grounds – from sports days and school fêtes to changes in the trees and flowers. There are different ways pupils could record these events. Some suggestions are given below:

- Pupils can keep diaries and journals about things that they do or see outside in their school grounds. Return to these on a regular basis in class so that they build a record of the school year. Reflect on these at the end of the year and discuss what has happened over that time. You may like to continue this from one year to the next and note the differences between the years as pupils move up the school.
- Looking from here …. Pupils are asked to find one particular view across their grounds or looking beyond the boundaries of the school. Throughout the year they return to this specific space and note the changes and activities they see. They could illustrate their writing with drawings or photographs.
- The sporting year is a good theme for journalistic writing. Sports will change each term and match reports can be written about games in lessons or between different classes or schools.

Art and design

Equipment required in addition to that listed above:

- sketchbooks, pencils, rubbers, crayons or paints and brushes;
- access to natural materials found at different times of year;
- large sheets of paper such as wallpaper or lining paper.

Description of the activity:

For your first art and design activity see the 'Sketching the seasons' activity in the 'Art and design' activities.

Throughout the year pupils will have access to different types of natural materials and therefore be able to create art that reflects seasonal change. Below are a few ideas to get you started using different natural materials throughout the year:

- Snow, even in very small amounts, is a great material for making marks in. Encourage pupils to use their own bodies, fingers or feet and see how many different ways they can make marks in the snow. They might try making patterns or pictures by jumping around, sliding their arms in the snow to make a snow angel, or making holes in the snow with their fingers.
- Flowers and seeds reflect the colours and shapes of the seasons. Use these to make patterns and pictures laid out on the ground or on sheets of paper to give a clear backdrop to the work. They could use some of the features in their grounds such as trees, people or buildings as their subjects.

Geography

Equipment required in addition to that listed above:

- clipboards and pencils, whiteboard and marker;
- thermometers, such as temperature guns and other weather equipment if you have it.

Description of the activity:

We now know that climate change is happening and that we are likely to see changes in the weather over the next few years. This activity helps pupils understand the difference between climate and weather.

The climate can be defined as the long-term pattern of weather in a particular area whilst the weather is what happens there from day to day. You can understand this better by looking at some of the micro-climates in your school grounds. Every space in the grounds has its own unique mini or 'micro-climate'. These will all be slightly different, just as every country in the world, every nation in the UK or every county or shire within each nation has a different climate.

- In groups, pupils select a place or space they are going to monitor over the school year.
- Each month measure specific elements of the weather in each space throughout a day, for example every hour. These should include:
    - noting when the sun is shining in that spot;
    - recording the temperature of the ground and/or the air temperature 1 metre above the ground (use a temperature gun to measure the ground temperature and a standard thermometer 1m above the ground for the air temperature);
    - if it is raining, seeing if puddles appear/disappear throughout the day;
    - if there is snow, ice or frost, seeing whether this disappears throughout the day;
    - noting how windy it is.
- Record your measurements on a graph and compare the variations between the different locations over the course of a year. This is like comparing different climates in different countries. The 'weather' was what it was like each time you went outside to take measurements, the 'micro-climates' were how different each space was over a year. Some may have been hotter all year, others hottest at one time of year and coldest at another.

It is not just the weather that changes throughout the year. Choose features or views to monitor over the seasons to record that change. Below are some things you might like to look at:

- How much do plants, including trees, grow over the year? Are there times of year when things grow more than other times?
- Do you see the impact of the weathering or other forms of erosion on some of the features in your school grounds? Has paint started to peel off railings or window frames? Has a muddy pathway been made across an area of grass by constant use?
- Are there puddles in different places when it rains? How quickly do these disappear? Where does the water go to? Are their drains or does it evaporate? Discuss the water cycle.

Cooking

Equipment required in addition to that listed above:

- something you can harvest from your own school grounds ideally;
- seasonal ingredients from the shops can be used as a supplement;
- campfire or stove and cooking equipment, including a source of water, something with which to handle hot items, as well as plates to eat off;
- a first-aid kit that includes something for dressing burns;
- information on different festivals and the food used within these celebrations.

Description of the activity:

These days we can access different fruit and vegetables throughout the year. However, this means that food either has to travel a long way to get here (being grown in another country where the climate or seasons are different) or be grown in the UK using artificial methods of heating and watering (that is, using extra fuel), or be stored for a long time (also using more fuel).

Instead, consider using seasonal ingredients for your campfire cooking. Discuss why this matters – talk about food miles and food production, as well as ways food can be stored to make it last longer. You may even want to investigate how this was done in the past before people had the refrigeration systems we have now.

Pupils may not know which fruit and vegetables are seasonal in this country. Planning your food-growing area will help them understand when crops will be ready to harvest. Make a selection so that you will have all the ingredients you need to make a seasonal recipe. Soups and roasted vegetables are a good way to use the crops you grow in meals that you can share around the campfire.

A great way to celebrate the seasons is to cook and eat festival food. This can be done in combination with the festivals activities outlined in the 'Religious and moral education' section above, or create your own school festival with music, art and drama.

Cook a selection of festival food outside, using crops you have grown yourselves where possible. Add to these, recipes cooked inside or celebration food brought into school, and take your celebrations outdoors.

Progression and extensions:

This theme is one that can be repeated each year – especially if you are going to introduce a calendar of special occasions into the school year.

Pupils in each year group could create their own events, add them to a school calendar and invite guests into the school to help make the days particularly special.

Adaptations:

If you don't have space, equipment or skills to cook outside, take this aspect inside then move outdoors to enjoy the celebrations and eating what you have made.

You may also like to think about using a space that you can walk to for some or all of your activities and even compare these with spaces within your grounds. This could be done by different year groups, with older pupils walking to a site and younger pupils using spaces within the grounds for their studies.

The Vikings have arrived

Subject areas:

- History and cooking
    - researching and cooking Viking food
- History and religious and moral education
    - how Vikings got along with their neighbours
- History and design and technology
    - about Viking housing
- History and art and design
    - about Viking clothes, textiles and crafts
- History and language and literacy
    - learning from Viking storytelling and listening

- History and PE
  - some Viking games

Key focus: A cross-curricula theme focusing on the Vikings

Level: Suitable across different levels, choose and adapt to fit your needs

Previous learning required:

A basic knowledge and understanding of Viking settlement and life in Britain.

Aim of the activity:

To take a thematic approach which actively explores Viking life in Britain using your school grounds as an energising space for learning and developing real-life skills.

Equipment:

Each activity has separate equipment requirements.

Description of the activity:

History themes enable investigations of aspects of real life in a hands-on way and this lends itself to cross-curricular learning. This series of Viking-based activities has relevance for literacy, art and design, maths, food technology, science, citizenship, environmental themes and even PE.

1. What did the Vikings eat for breakfast?
2. Did they get on with their neighbours?
3. Would I feel at home in a Viking house?
4. Clothes, textiles and crafts
5. Storytelling and writing
6. Viking PE and games

History and cookery: what did Vikings eat for breakfast?

Equipment required in addition to that listed above:

- mixing bowls;
- camp stove (or open fire);
- cast iron pan or griddle;

- weighing scales;
- wooden spoon and teaspoons;
- water;
- barley flour, wholemeal flour, crushed flax seeds, butter, salt, honey;
- a first-aid kit for working around a fire.

Description of the activity:

The joy of outdoor cooking with simple recipes is that there is less clearing up to do and it is more authentic to the period. If you do not have outdoor tables or benches you could set up a temporary outdoor, camp-style kitchen with tarpaulins to sit on.

The Vikings made several kinds of bread and the following recipe is for flat-bread cooked in a cast iron pan:

Prepare the Viking bread by mixing the following quantities in a bowl: 150g barley flour, 50g wholemeal flour, 2tsps flax seeds, a knob of butter, a pinch of salt and enough water to make a good dough. Knead the dough for a few minutes and then cover and leave aside for about an hour. When ready, take handfuls of dough, roll them into balls and flatten them to about 1cm thick. Cook in a dry cast-iron pan for a few minutes on each side.

The Vikings would eat them with honey.

Progression and extensions:

- Pupils could compare the flavour and texture to modern day breads.
- There are several Viking porridge recipes that could be experimented with using different kinds of grains and additions such as chopped apples.

History and religious and moral education: did they get on with their neighbours?

Equipment required in addition to that listed above:

- props suitable for role play;
- vocabulary cards;
- role cards;
- clipboard, pencils and paper or whiteboard and markers.

Description of the activity:

Being both raiders and settlers, the Vikings brought some new ways of doing things to Britain. As with all village communities, arguments could break out between neighbours over things such as when a person's livestock had trampled a neighbour's crop. There are some great drama and debate possibilities that could be enacted in the school grounds, against a backdrop chosen by your pupils.

- Set up a television interview between a modern person and a Viking. It could be a news interview around an important event or a feature about an aspect of Viking lifestyle or culture. Pupils can frame the questions they want to ask and what answers to provide.
- Ask pupils to imagine a dispute between Viking and Anglo-Saxon neighbours, one that needs a village meeting to resolve it. Roles can be assigned and pupils given a brief about their likely point of view. Pupils could be encouraged to use Viking and Anglo-Saxon vocabulary (such as 'thane' and 'thrall') and names, by having some word and name cards for pupils to choose and use. Choosing a setting outdoors will be part of the task.
- Hold a debate about women's and men's rights in Viking and Anglo-Saxon society. Pupils could find stones to use as tokens for when they are speaking.

History and design and technology: would I feel at home in a Viking house?

Equipment required in addition to that listed above:

- chalk;
- tape measures;
- tarpaulins, clips, ropes and a mallet;
- buckets and water;
- hazel poles, bendy sticks (e.g. willow), sticky mud, straw or turf;
- pictures of longhouses.

Description of the activity:

Viking longhouses were impressive in scale and distinctive in the ways they were lived in. Here are a few ideas for exploring whether you would feel at home in a Viking house or not.

- To get a sense of scale and the shape of longhouses, pupils could measure and mark out the floorplan of a typical one (around 6 metres wide and anywhere from 15 to 75 metres long, all on one level). This could be compared with the footprint of an average modern house (90 metres squared and usually two storeys), leading to some calculations and discussion of differences in design and how spaces were used. Another option is to use tarpaulins to create the footprints of both kinds of homes and then enjoy some longhouse den-building.
- Longhouses were made from gathered materials: wood, mud, straw and turf. Miniature or knee-high houses could be built by pupils making a wooden frame of hazel poles for the outer walls and for the two interior lines of roof supports running the length of the inside.

The walls can be panelled with wattle, by weaving bendy sticks across and then adding draught-excluding sticky mud. Floors can be pounded down by the stamping of feet and the roof covered with more hazel poles or sticks and straw thatch or pieces of turf. No windows are needed and gaps in the roof act as a chimney. Pupils can experience collecting some of the building materials and experimenting with techniques to make the house solid and weatherproof.

History and art and design: clothes, textiles and crafts

Equipment required in addition to that listed above:

- yarn or string for weaving (random colours from charity shops would be good);
- rectangles of strong cardboard;
- scissors and pinking shears;
- sticky tape;
- photographs of Viking brooches, amulets and chess-pieces from archaeological sites;
- clay and tools for clay-working;
- junk materials such as old packaging;
- glue and masking tape;
- paint and brushes.

Description of the activity:

Many of the crafts that the Vikings perfected can be tried outdoors using simple materials. This will provide an authentic understanding of how people often took their work outside and used materials they found there.

- Simple weaving looms can be made by taking a rectangle of thick cardboard and cutting notches along the top and bottom edges or using pinking shears. The warp yarn should be wound around in a continuous piece, sitting in the notches and secured by tape at the cut ends. Pupils can use coloured yarn or string for the weft to create patterns. The finished piece can be cut from the loom and displayed or sewn up to make a small pouch.
- Viking brooches and amulets (good luck charms) had a distinctive style and were considered useful: brooches for securing cloaks and amulets for keeping people safe. Pupils could design and make Viking-inspired items from clay, based on photographs of archaeological finds.
- The prows of Viking longboats featuring heads of dragons, serpents and other mythical beasts could make an inspiring project, using junk materials to create a large-scale replica or pupils' own individual designs. For small-scale versions, pupils could use bread dough which can be baked, or clay which can be left to dry before painting.

Progression and extensions:

- Play with the nettle patch! Make nettle dye to add a golden colour to neutral-coloured yarn for weaving – and maybe a red onion skin dye too. The Vikings used many wildflowers that are in short supply today, so instead, use things that are easily available. Pupils can also make string from nettle stems and soup from the leaves. Use gloves when picking and working with the nettles.

History and language and literacy: storytelling and writing

Equipment required in addition to that listed above:

- examples of Viking sagas for reading out loud;
- a campfire setting;
- crepe paper for flames if you are not building a real fire;
- writing materials;
- images of the runic alphabet;
- charcoal;
- vegetable oil;
- plastic yoghurt pots;
- sticks;
- paint brushes.

Description of the activity:

Campfire story time is something the Vikings perfected to a fine art with their sagas, told through the long, dark days and nights of their homeland.

- After hearing some sagas read aloud and having been introduced to some of the characters, pupils could write their own mini-sagas and perform them around a campfire setting. If the campfire is not real, create the same atmosphere by having pupils collect sticks and build a fire with flames made from crepe paper. Pupils could also play a Chinese whispers game to see how oral storytelling allows for changes over time.
- The Viking runic alphabet can be used for some literacy activities. Pupils could write their name, or a message, in runes using found objects like sticks and stones and scoring the runes onto stones or painting them onto pebbles.
- With home-made charcoal paint (made using crushed charcoal and a little vegetable oil), pupils could pair up and see how many different words they can make from their runes. Each word can be recorded by photographing or writing it down, before mixing the runes up to have another go.

History and PE: Viking PE and games

Equipment needed in addition to that listed above:

- loose parts such as crates, tarps, poles and ropes;
- chalk and tape measures;
- PVC piping approximately 1m x 1.5cm, in which you have already drilled or melted a hole at either end for threading string through;
- strong string;
- squares of foam;
- bamboo canes cut to arrow length and with a notch cut at one end;
- pieces of felt, gaffer tape and elastic bands;
- circles of wood or thick cardboard around 20cm diameter;
- some fabric tied up into an apple-sized soft ball.

Description of the activity:

Physical strength and teamwork were important in Viking culture, with the traditions of rowing and throwing. These battle-inspired Viking actions allow history-themed opportunities for PE lessons.

- Longboats and rowing: some Viking longboats were powered by hundreds of rowers, paired side-by-side. Pupils could either make a whole-class loose parts longboat or they could measure and mark out a longboat and each set of oars in chalk on the playground, or with ropes and short sticks on the grass. Then as a class, try keeping in time with the motions of rowing. Ask pupils to think of techniques for keeping in time with each other and try them out, for example chanting some phrases they have made up, singing a song they all know, or someone banging a rhythm. Discuss what would happen if one side stopped rowing and the other side carried on. What else would they like to find out about longboats?
- Viking children had a selection of games to play. Some were straightforward skills-based competitions, like archery, axe throwing and spear throwing. To make a bow and arrow, tie a knot at one end of the string and thread it through one of the PVC piping holes and pull it through, then thread it through the hole at the other end and pull it taught until the piping bends to make a bow shape. Tie a knot to secure the string in place. Cut a piece of foam and tape it halfway down the curve of the bow, to make a handhold and arrow rest. Make an arrow with a cane by taping over the end without the notch and securing a piece of felt over it with an elastic band, making a firm but safe arrow. Pupils can practise shooting at targets they have made. For spear-throwing, hazel poles can be used. There is scope for trial and error, pupils sharing tips about how they think it works best and for teaching javelin techniques. Pupils could approximate axe-throwing techniques using sticks that they have weighted at one end with plasticine, so the stick will spin like an axe when thrown at a tree trunk.

- A Viking bat and ball game called 'Kingybats' is good for skill and patience. Pupils stand in a circle, each holding a round bat of wood or thick cardboard which they use to pass a ball of tied fabric round without letting it fall on the ground. Pupils could speculate and test how they think the Viking children played this, as it might have included batting the fabric ball around the circle. Does it remind them of any games they already know? Could they devise their own games with similar materials?

Biodiversity in our school grounds

Key focus: From surveying school grounds for biodiversity to making changes to encourage more wildlife in your grounds, whilst also reinforcing learning on biodiversity.

Curriculum areas covered:

- Science
    - researching the life cycles of local wildlife
    - habitats
    - presenting findings
- Language and literacy
    - descriptive language
    - researching using different sources and identifying fact
    - writing for different audiences and for different reasons

- Design and technology
    - research, design and build a product
- Art and design
    - illustration – drawing skills
    - creating models
- Geography
    - habitat mapping

Level: All – find the activities that work best for your class

Previous learning required:

An understanding of what wildlife might live locally.
What we mean by: life cycles, habitat, food source.

Aim of the activity:

To undertake a cross-curricula project on the theme of biodiversity and to reinforce scientific learning. To include surveying the school grounds and improving habitats and food sources for the benefit of wildlife.

Equipment (across all curriculum areas):

- clipboards, paper and pencils;
- information about local wildlife, for example insects and other invertebrates, amphibians, small mammals;
- see also each curriculum area for additional specific equipment needed.

Description of the activity:

Whilst the main and most obvious curriculum focus for biodiversity is science, this theme is one that can be taken across many different curriculum areas.

This is a great theme for environmentally concerned pupils and staff as biodiversity matters and you can help to make a difference.

An introduction to biodiversity:

Check out the latest 'State of Nature' report to get the latest information about wildlife in the UK. It will tell you which plants and animals are at risk, whether there have been increases or decreases in wildlife populations across the UK and why these changes have happened. The report covers the whole of the UK and also breaks down the information by nation. From this you can pick out some key facts to use with your pupils as a starting point for investigating the biodiversity in your own school grounds.

Science

Equipment required in addition to that listed above:

- printed resources or website links providing information about a selection of different UK animals that can be found in your area, especially those that live in, or could live in, your school grounds;
- many organisations provide information on different plants and animals – some will be local, others national, some will focus on a specific animal or type, for example mammals or hedgehogs, whilst others will be there to protect all types of wildlife or plants;
- plans of your school grounds.

In the progressions and extensions section of this activity there is information about how to run a more in-depth project on the biodiversity of your school grounds. However, if you don't want to go into that depth but still want to teach pupils about wildlife, here are some science activities that can help you on your way.

- Pupils choose an animal to research from a list of species common to your area. You can provide a limited list with information but do make sure there is a good variety within the class so that not everyone researches the same thing!
- Pupils can survey their grounds for different habitats and food sources and see if they are suitable for the animal they have chosen to research, for example are there good habitats and food sources for them? From this they can make suggestions about what changes could be made to the grounds to encourage more of their species of animal to live there.
- Pupils can present their findings to the rest of the class and discuss what changes would be most beneficial for different wildlife.

Language and literacy

Equipment required in addition to that listed above:

- information about and pictures of local wildlife either online or from books;
- blank pieces of card to draw and write descriptions of their creatures on.

As well as researching information about local wildlife from websites and books, pupils can write about them in a range of ways. Here are some ideas to get you started:

- Pupils play 'guess who' or 'top trumps' using descriptions of their chosen creatures. Through this they will develop their scientific vocabulary as they learn to describe the features of different animals. Consider descriptions of colour, shape, size, wings, eyes, antennae, legs, life cycle, food and habitat. Each pupil can research these features so as to build a complete set for the class to play with.
- Pupils can write about a chosen animal visiting your grounds to see if they want to live there. They can describe the habitats in your grounds, what food they might like to eat, what they might see when they visit.
- Pupils can write the text for interpretation boards or information sheets on the insects found in your grounds.

Design and technology

Equipment required in addition to that listed above:

This will depend on what type of habitat you want to build.

For a bug hotel

A framework for your bug hotel such as wooden pallets, bricks with holes in, sticks, bamboo, straw, mud, leaves, moss and other natural materials, terracotta pots, planks of wood.

- Research, design and build bug hotels and other habitats for your chosen insects. There are many guides online on how to make a bug hotel, but don't forget these need to be refurbished regularly over the winter months to prevent disease spreading in your pollinating insects.
- Other habitats and food sources include herb or vegetable beds, orchards (five or more fruit trees), hedges, meadows or bee banks.

For bird, bat or hedgehog boxes

- Search online or contact your local wildlife organisation to help you discover what you need to make these habitats for your school grounds. There are many different versions, so maybe research these as part of your lesson and decide as a class which you want to try out – you might even compare different designs.

Art and design

Equipment required in addition to that listed above:

- art materials that will last outside for interpretation boards;
- a selection of recycled materials, for example carboard boxes and tubes, netting, pipes and gutters, pipe cleaners, etc.

Illustrate the new interpretation boards about the animals that live in your grounds, so that everyone in your school and visitors to your grounds also learn about the importance of biodiversity and how you are helping to increase this.

Use recycled materials to create giant versions of your chosen animals, maybe at different stages in their life cycles. Place these in the habitat in which they live in real life.

Geography

Equipment required in addition to that listed above:

- Maps of your grounds.

Create a habitat map of your grounds. See the National Education Nature Park guidance for more details of how to map the biodiversity in your school grounds.

Talk with the grounds staff about how they manage the different habitats and maybe even encourage them to change the way they cut the grass, manage weeds (stop using pesticides) or choose pollinator-friendly plants when they add new plants to the grounds.

Progression and extensions:

We have created five activities under this theme, but there are many more things you could do if this is a topic you would like to look at in more detail. You can help add data to the UK Pollinator Monitoring Scheme (PoMS) by surveying your grounds to see which insects live in or visit your grounds. Search for the X-Polli:Nation project website to access more information and guidance or search for the Polli:Nation project on the Learning through Landscapes website for even more resources and information.

As with other aspects of this activity, local and national wildlife organisations will be able to tell you about schemes you can add your data to – including the National Education Nature Park data.

Adaptations:

Consider improving your grounds for wildlife, using the research from this theme. This can be as simple as letting grass grow long on your field or adding pots of plants to a barren playground. Keep re-doing your wildlife surveys to see if you increase the wildlife in your grounds over the years.

17
Other useful resources

- More information about Learning through Landscapes (LtL), our training and resources can be found on our website at www.ltl.org.uk. This includes:
  - information about how to become a member and receive our digital newsletter, keeping you up to date with how we can support you better;
  - free downloadable learning resources;
  - links to our on-line training programme;
  - information on grants and projects for schools;
  - All our Risk Benefit Assessments and policy documents are available on our website. Please look for the section on managing risk.

If you struggle to find what you need, email us on enquiries@ltl.org.uk

- If you have been inspired to take more of your teaching outside you may find the LtL '… in the school grounds' series useful. Published between 1992 and 2001, they are full of ideas that are still relevant for teaching outdoors. Search online for the following titles:
  - *Science in the school grounds*
  - *Mathematics in the school grounds*
  - *English in the school grounds*
  - *History in the school grounds*
  - *Geography in the school grounds*
  - *Arts in the school grounds*
  - *Personal, Social and Health Education in the school grounds*
  - *Physical Education in the school grounds*

- If you are looking for in-depth and structured schemes of work for outdoor learning across the curriculum you will find *The National Curriculum Outdoors* published by Bloomsbury Education helpful.

- Juliet Robertson's organisation Creative Star has both books and a website that promote and support innovative and creative outdoor learning and play in the early years and primary schools.
- *Learning in the Outdoor Classroom* is a Swedish anthology of outdoor learning activities published by OutdoorTeacherFölag AB with ideas for both primary and secondary pupils.
- To learn more about the benefits of managed risk in school grounds, visit the International School Grounds Alliance website to see their declaration on risk in school grounds.
- The UK Health and Safety Executive have excellent advice for school trips, please visit their website and search for the education section.
- If you are interested in developing a whole school approach to outdoor learning then there is no better book than *The Coombes Approach,* written by two of the head teachers, Susan Rowe and Susan Humphries, from Coombes Infant School. This book will inspire and inform your philosophy and approach.
- For more tools and support for using local spaces outside your school grounds, we recommend the 'Beyond your Boundary' resource published by Nature Scot.
- There are new apps being developed all the time, so we have not provided a list here as it would soon be out of date! But do search for the following types of app that you may find useful:
  - weather apps to both tell you when it might be best to go outside (or not) and to help you measure the conditions when outdoors;
  - animal and plant identification apps;
  - mapping apps;
  - sound, image and video recording and editing apps;
  - apps that measure heights, distances and time;
  - apps that allow for your pupils to interact with you and each other, for example through voting, submitting information or sharing images;
  - apps that create QR codes;
  - apps that can identify the pitch or volume of sounds;
  - apps that can determine air quality.

- There is one app we will be more specific about. The Learning through Landscapes school grounds audit tool will help you assess the quality of your grounds and your existing provision for outdoor learning and play. Find out more on our website in the resources section.
- Check out policy and guidance from your own nation's education department. These are continually being added to and include:
  - The Learning Estate Strategy from the Scottish Government, the 21st Century Schools programme from the Welsh Government and Every School a Good School from the Education Department of Northern Ireland.

Index

Locators in **bold** refer to tables and those in *italics* to figures. Activity names are indicated by single quote marks ('Activity').

accessibility 24–25
activities for curriculum teaching 29–30; *see also* arts activities; humanities activities; language/literacy activities; maths activities; science activities; technology activities
air quality 21
angles activity 76–77
art galleries 193–194
arts activities 156–172; 'Biodiversity in our school grounds' 232–233; 'Dig for Victory' 210–211; 'Grow, cook, eat, celebrate!' 203–204; 'Outdoor artist inspiration' 160–165; 'Performance makers' 169–171; 'Seasonal change' 217–218; 'Sketching out the seasons' 157–159; 'Sounds around our grounds' 166–168; themes 172

bar charts activity 74–75
behaviour management 22–23
'Biodiversity in our school grounds' 229–233
'Building a bridge over a puddle' 177–179
'Building Bronze Age dens' 148–149

'Circle debate' 35–37
circles activities 78–83
climate change 12
clothing, dressing for the weather 15–16
computer technology 173
cooking 173; 'Dig for Victory' 210; 'Grow, cook, eat, celebrate!' 198–205; 'Seasonal change' 219–220; 'The Vikings have arrived' 221–228
'Could an animal live here?' 111–113
'Crazy golf' 174–176
'Create a game' 45–47
'Creating a compass' 98–100
curriculum teaching 29–30, 234–235; *see also* arts activities; humanities activities; language/literacy activities; maths activities; science activities; technology activities

dance activity 169–171
debating activity 35–37
'Den dimensions' 69–70
descriptive language 43–44
design and technology activities *see* technology activities
diary activity 48–49
'Dig for Victory' 206–212
digestive system activity 120–122
disabled access 24–25
'Discovering pi' 81–83
drama activity 169–171

'Eco-activists' 50–52
effective learning 22, 26
environment: 'Biodiversity in our school grounds' 229–233; 'Could an animal live here?' 111–113; pollution 21; 'Sketching out the seasons' 157–159; sustainability 12; 'Wildlife champions' 114–116
equipment: appropriate for the weather 15–16; list of 17–18, *18*; maintaining an inventory 26; sourcing 17; storage **11**
experts, bringing in 194–195
'Exploring angles' 76–77
'Exploring labyrinths' 153–155
'Exploring number and place value through natural materials' 89–93

filming activity 191–192
'Find a tree' 43–44
'Folding fractions' 84–85
'Follow that …' 130–131
'Following and listening to clues' 32–34
food technology 173
fractions activities 84–88
friction activity 101–103

games activities 45–47, 227–228
gardening activities: 'Dig for Victory' 206–212; 'Grow, cook, eat, celebrate!' 198–205

gathering space **9**
geography activities 129; 'Biodiversity in our school grounds' 233; 'Follow that …' 130–131; 'It's how hot?' 138–140; 'Seasonal change' 218–219; 'The travelling fruit' 132–134; 'What makes our school grounds special?' 135–137
grounds 8; learning off-site 14; seating and gathering **9**; shade and shelter **10**; small spaces 13–14; storage **11**; sustainability 12; 'What makes our school grounds special?' 135–137
'Grow, cook, eat, celebrate!' 198–205

habitats activity 111–113
history activities 129; 'Building Bronze Age dens' 148–149; 'Dig for Victory' 208; 'History under the ground' 143–144; 'Oldest and newest' 141–142; 'Our class timeline' 145–147; 'The Vikings have arrived' 221–228
'History under the ground' 143–144
humanities activities 129–155; 'Building Bronze Age dens' 148–149; 'Exploring labyrinths' 153–155; 'Follow that …' 130–131; 'History under the ground' 143–144; 'It's how hot?' 138–140; 'Oldest and newest' 141–142; 'Our class timeline' 145–147; 'Sensing a story' 150–152; 'The travelling fruit' 132–134; themes 155; 'What makes our school grounds special?' 135–137
'The human bar chart' 74–75
'A hunt for the truth' 53–54

inclusion 24–25
information sharing techniques 190–191
information technology 173
'It's how hot?' 138–140

language/literacy activities 31–62; 'A hunt for the truth' 53–54; 'Biodiversity in our school grounds' 231–232; 'Circle debate' 35–37; 'Create a game' 45–47; 'Dig for Victory' 211–212; 'Eco-activists' 50–52; 'Find a tree' 43–44; 'Following and listening to clues' 32–34; 'Grow, cook, eat, celebrate!' 201–202; 'Leaf descriptions' 41–42; 'My outdoor diary' 48–49; 'Reading from a range of texts outdoors' 57–61; 'Reflecting on outdoor experiences' 55–56; 'Seasonal change' 217; 'Sensing a story' 150–152; 'Story stones' 38–40; 'The Vikings have arrived' 226; themes 62
'Leaf descriptions' 41–42
learning outcomes 22
learning outdoors *see* outdoor learning
Learning through Landscapes (LtL) resources 234–235
literacy *see* language/literacy activities

'Making rainbows' 109–110
maps activities 130–137

maths activities 63–93; 'Den dimensions' 69–70; 'Discovering pi' 81–83; 'Exploring angles' 76–77; 'Exploring number and place value through natural materials' 89–93; 'Folding fractions' 84–85; 'Grow, cook, eat, celebrate!' 201; 'Measuring outdoor circles' 78–80; 'Outdoor number lines' 64–66; 'Size comparisons' 67–68; 'Stick fraction walls' 86–88; 'The human bar chart' 74–75; themes 93; 'Various volumes' 71–73
'Measuring outdoor circles' 78–80
modern foreign languages 211
museums 193–194
music activities 156; 'Performance makers' 169–171; 'Understanding how sound can change in both volume and pitch' 123–128
'My outdoor diary' 48–49
myth busting *27*

natural materials 17; 'Exploring number and place value through natural materials' 89–93; 'Find a tree' 43–44; 'Leaf descriptions' 41–42; 'Outdoor artist inspiration' 160–165; 'Story stones' 38–40; using loose parts 192–193; 'What's this made of?' 104–106
nature as stimulus 31
number lines activity 64–66
numeracy *see* maths activities

off-site space 14
'Oldest and newest' 141–142
'Our class timeline' 145–147
'Outdoor artist inspiration' 160–165
outdoor learning: planning your journey 3–7, *5*, *6*, *28*; why take learning outdoors? *4*
'Outdoor number lines' 64–66
outdoor space *see* grounds; off-site space

'Parachutes away!' 95–97
'Performance makers' 169–171
physical education activity 227–228
pi 81–83
place value 89–93
planning your journey 3–7, *5*, *6*, *28*
pollution 21
postbox revision 189–190
pupil behaviour 22–23
pupils' work, presentation of 195–196

'Quick activities' 184–188

rainbows activity 109–110
'Reading from a range of texts outdoors' 57–61
recording equipment 17
'Reflecting on outdoor experiences' 55–56
religious education activities 129; 'Exploring labyrinths' 153–155; 'Grow, cook, eat, celebrate!' 204;

'Seasonal change' 216; 'Sensing a story' 150–152; 'The Vikings have arrived' 223–224
resources, other useful resources 234–235
revision techniques 189–190, 196
risk 19–21, *20*
risk assessment 19
risk-benefit approach *20*

school grounds audit tool 8; *see also* grounds
science activities 94–128; 'Biodiversity in our school grounds' 229–233; 'Could an animal live here?' 111–113; 'Creating a compass' 98–100; 'Dig for Victory' 209–210; 'Grow, cook, eat, celebrate!' 200; 'Making rainbows' 109–110; 'Parachutes away!' 95–97; 'Seasonal change' 213–220; themes 128; 'Understanding how sound can change in both volume and pitch' 123–128; 'Using my senses' 117–119; 'Walking the digestive system' 120–122; 'What's this made of?' 104–106; 'Where's the water gone?' 107–108; 'Why won't it move?' 101–103; 'Wildlife champions' 114–116
'Seasonal change' 213–220
seasons activities 157–159, 213–220
seating **9**
senses activity 117–119
'Sensing a story' 150–152
shade **10**
shelter **10**
'Size comparisons' 67–68
'Sketching out the seasons' 157–159
small spaces 13–14
sounds activities 123–128, 156, 166–168
'Sounds around our grounds' 166–168
space *see* grounds; off-site space
'Stick fraction walls' 86–88
storage **11**

'Story stones' 38–40
sustainability 12; 'Eco-activists' activity 50–52

technology activities 173–179; 'Biodiversity in our school grounds' 232; 'Building a bridge over a puddle' 177–179; 'Crazy golf' 174–176; 'Dig for Victory' 209; 'The Vikings have arrived' 224–226; themes 179
texts for outdoor reading 57–61
'The travelling fruit' 132–134
themes, teaching through 197; 'Biodiversity in our school grounds' 229–233; 'Dig for Victory' 206–212; 'Grow, cook, eat, celebrate!' 198–205; 'Seasonal change' 213–220; 'The Vikings have arrived' 221–228
time constraints, making time for outdoor learning 23

'Understanding how sound can change in both volume and pitch' 123–128
'Using my senses' 117–119

'Various volumes' 71–73
'The Vikings have arrived' 221–228
volumes activity 71–73

'Walking the digestive system' 120–122
water cycle activity 107–108
weather 15–16
'What makes our school grounds special?' 135–137
'What's this made of?' 104–106
'Where's the water gone?' 107–108
'Why won't it move?' 101–103
'Wildlife champions' 114–116
writing equipment 17; *see also* language/literacy activities
written evidence of learning 22